ASHE Higher Education Report
Kelly Ward, Lisa E. Wolf-Wendel, Serie

MW01051897

Women's Status in Higher Education: Equity Matters

Elizabeth J. Allan

Women's Status in Higher Education: Equity Matters
Elizabeth J. Allan
ASHE Higher Education Report: Volume 37, Number 1
Kelly Ward, Lisa E. Wolf-Wendel, Series Editors

ISSN 1551-6970   electronic ISSN 1554-6306   ISBN 978-1-1180-7334-6

The **ASHE Higher Education Report** is part of the Jossey-Bass Higher and Adult Education Series and is published six times a year by Wiley Subscription Services, Inc., A Wiley Company, at Jossey-Bass, 989 Market Street, San Francisco, California 94103-1741.

For subscription information, see the Back Issue/Subscription Order Form in the back of this volume.

CALL FOR PROPOSALS: Prospective authors are strongly encouraged to contact Kelly Ward (kaward@wsu.edu) or Lisa Wolf-Wendel (lwolf@ku.edu). See "About the ASHE Higher Education Report Series" in the back of this volume.

Visit the Jossey-Bass Web site at **www.josseybass.com.**

Printed in the United States of America on acid-free recycled paper.

The **ASHE Higher Education Report** is indexed in CIJE: Current Index to Journals in Education (ERIC), Current Abstracts (EBSCO), Education Index/Abstracts (H.W. Wilson), ERIC Database (Education Resources Information Center), Higher Education Abstracts (Claremont Graduate University), IBR & IBZ: International Bibliographies of Periodical Literature (K.G. Saur), and Resources in Education (ERIC).

Advisory Board

The ASHE Higher Education Report Series is sponsored by the Association for the Study of Higher Education (ASHE), which provides an editorial advisory board of ASHE members.

Contents

Executive Summary

Significant gains have been made in women's access to and representation in higher education. Although they are important, focus on these improvements provides only a partial picture of gender equity and inequity. Taken alone, enrollment data tend to eclipse other factors that shape women's experiences in higher education. For instance, aggregate enrollment data do not portray the persistent lack of gender parity among students studying engineering, computer science, and other science and technology fields, nor do they depict the quality of classroom and campus experiences. Women studying and working in postsecondary institutions continue to bump against glass ceilings and sticky floors, they experience pay disparities and the threat and reality of sexual harassment, and violence continues to interfere with workplace and living environments on campus.

Why Should We Care?

Lack of equity in higher education can have far-reaching and negative consequences for learning environments, quality of life, and career satisfaction of both women and men studying and working in academic institutions. This monograph foregrounds gains made and shared challenges women face while also acknowledging how race, social class, and other aspects of identity intersect with sex and gender and contribute to shaping one's professional status in profound ways. Literature related to women's access and representation in higher education, experiences of campus climate, and predominant strategies employed to enhance gender equity in U.S. higher education are reviewed.

Analyzing Power and Change

A range of theoretical frames in feminism offers diverse approaches to conceptualizing power, understanding complexities of inequity, and advancing strategies for change. Feminist theories developed and refined over the last century provide a set of lenses to analyze oppression and promote equity in a range of contexts, including higher education. This monograph makes the case that drawing on a range of diverse feminist theories can help broaden and deepen analysis of persistent equity problems and, in turn, enhance the likelihood of finding more effective solutions.

Access and Representation

The greatest movement toward numerical parity is among students, where women currently account for 57 percent of undergraduates and are pursuing degrees in a range of disciplines across virtually every type of postsecondary institution. In fact, women have become the majority of degree earners in nearly every level of postsecondary education, except Ph.D. and M.D. programs (King, 2010). It remains the case, however, that women are heavily concentrated in particular fields, earning a majority of their degrees in health professions, psychology, education, other social sciences, and the humanities. Patterns of inequity are typically amplified for women of color. Lack of parity also is noted in research related to student engagement and cocurricular activities, including athletics.

Representation of faculty, staff, and administrators reflects persistent gaps in equity for women in higher-ranking positions such as full professorships or provost and in doctoral-granting research universities. The same trends apply to the representation of women senior administrators, presidents, and members of governing boards (Cook and Cordova, 2007; Glazer-Raymo, 2008c; King and Gomez, 2008; Touchton, Musil, and Campbell, 2008).

Campus Climates

For women students, classroom climates, men's violence, harassment, and romance culture remain climate-related problems. For faculty, staff, and senior administrators, challenges related to work and family balance, the "ideal worker norm," conceptualizations of leadership, occupational segregation, and salary inequity are often additional problems. They are frequently compounded for women of color, first-generation women, lesbian, and disabled women, who must also navigate the climate-related challenges that emerge from workplaces and learning environments that privilege white, middle-class, able-bodied, and heterosexual norms. Expanded understandings of equity (those that incorporate campus climate) have called for expanded thinking and strategy development beyond increasing the numbers of women in the pipeline (White, 2005).

Strategies to Enhance Women's Status

A range of approaches exists for promoting gender equity in higher education. The review of change strategies, however, suggests a continued strong reliance on liberal feminist perspectives. Enhanced recruitment, increasing availability of team sports, implementation and enforcement of antidiscrimination policies, "grooming mentoring" and professional development to widen the pool of qualified applicants all reflect liberal feminist conceptualizations of power as a resource to be more evenly distributed between men and women in higher education.

Other types of feminist influences are evident in common strategies that include the establishment and support of women's student centers, women's colleges, feminist research and writing groups, advocacy of collective decision making and generative approaches to leadership, networks of women, a focus on community, and empowerment of women.

Recommendations

Much has been learned about women's status in higher education over the past two decades, yet further research is needed to analyze gaps across identity differences like race, sexual identity, and disability and to better understand factors that both impede and accelerate the pace of change along the path to truly equitable representation for all women students, staff, faculty, and administrators in higher education. Familiarity with a range of feminist theories can help broaden perspectives on power and causes of inequity and help expand change strategies.

Three key recommendations emerge from this analysis of the literature: (1) *Promote and support opportunities to learn more about women's experiences in general and in higher education in particular;* (2) *analyze gender equity problems and solutions through multiple feminist frames;* and (3) *develop and implement change strategies that reflect diverse feminist perspectives.* Analyzing the nature of inequity from multiple perspectives can help broaden the repertoire of strategies available to sustain current gains and ideally, increase the pace of change toward equity.

Foreword

Research related to women's issues in higher education often gets stuck at an impasse between parity and equity. Women have made great strides with regard to representation—accounting for the majority of undergraduates on many campuses, approaching equal numbers to men in many disciplines in graduate programs, making progress in the incoming faculty ranks, and striving for (and often achieving) greater representation as staff and administrators. What is often missing from pictures of numerical progress, however, is further examination of the larger landscape of equity and how women fare beyond the numbers.

Absent a critical examination of equity—what it means for women, how it is achieved, and why it is important for colleges and universities—it is easy to focus on the progress women have made in terms of representation and think ongoing work related to gender equity is done. Many colleges and universities have gotten lazy about attention to equity with regard to gender given the numerical progress women have made. Campus practitioners and faculty also often fail to consider how life and context are different for women with overlapping identities as people of color, differently abled, or with sexual identity that is not heterosexual. In many instances it is white women who have made the progress on college campuses, and failing to consider different aspects of identity, not just gender, provides an incomplete picture of the progress all women have made. The author is careful to consider different aspects of identity for women throughout the monograph. Allan's monograph provides much needed background, demographic information, and theoretical perspectives to more fully understand the relationship between equity and parity for all types of women in an effort to guide campuses in their work to establish and maintain focus on gender equity.

Elizabeth Allan does a masterful job of providing an overview of the role and status of women in higher education. She charts the progress women have made as undergraduates, graduate students, faculty, staff, and administrators. She also acknowledges the important role that campus climate and context play in establishing and maintaining diverse and equitable contexts for not just women but for all students, faculty, staff, and administrators.

Allan's approach is unique because it provides the background information and context as well as the theoretical tools necessary to dismantle and understand issues related to women and gender equity on campus. It is easy to look at aggregate numbers of women as students and faculty and see the progress women have made in all aspects of higher education (and good progress it has been). Absent the theoretical tools to analyze and critique women's progress, however, the focus on gender remains superficial by a limited focus on numerical progress. Superficial analysis also fails to consider context, climate, and different disciplinary and institutional contexts. Allan's use of theory introduces different feminist perspectives and shows how they are useful tools of analysis and understanding that go beyond the aggregate. Using a range of feminist theoretical perspectives, Allan equips readers with the necessary tools to analyze gender in a context of power and change.

The monograph is sure to be useful for practitioners and researchers alike as they grapple with the ongoing integration and progress of women in different campus domains. Staff members working specifically with programs (curricular and cocurricular) designed to meet the needs of female students are sure to find this monograph of use as they carry out their work and as they justify and explain, as they often have to do, the importance of programs that focus on the unique needs of women. Faculty and administrators concerned with maintaining quality and diverse students and faculty will also find the monograph useful, given the emphasis on context and women's representation at different levels of colleges and universities. Researchers interested in different aspects of gender equity will find the monograph helpful to tease out the nuances of gender and equity. The monograph is also sure to be a useful tool to those working in higher education as practitioners and researchers who want to be better equipped and conversant in how theory can be used to understand, explain, and critically analyze different phenomena in higher education.

The ASHE monograph series has not dedicated a volume to the examination of gender since the publication of Aguirre's *Women and Minority Faculty in the Academic Workplace: Recruitment, Retention, and Academic Culture* (2000). That volume was very comprehensive and important to facilitate understanding of issues facing women and minority faculty in higher education; however, the focus was limited to faculty. Although gender has not been the exclusive focus of a monograph in many years, the topic has been addressed in many other monographs, among them O'Meara, LaPointe Terosky, and Neumann's *Faculty Careers and Work Lives: A Professional Growth Perspective* (2009). Allan's monograph stands as a companion to many other volumes in the series.

Elizabeth Allan offers a very insightful, critical, and thorough analysis of literature related to women's role and status in higher education. Using theory, data, and existing research, Allan prompts all of us to think beyond normative perspectives of women's place and progress in higher education and challenges us to think critically about parity and work tirelessly for gender equity.

Kelly Ward
Series Editor

Acknowledgments

I have many special people to thank for helping me bring this project to fruition. First, my husband Brian provided steadfast support, nurturing, and encouragement along the way, and I thank him for always being there. Our children, ages 14, 11, 9, and 6, have grown and changed considerably since this book was initially conceptualized. They too have provided me support and inspiration for this work and much more. I thank my parents for encouraging my academic pursuits and for instilling a strong commitment to social justice that continues to fuel my research and writing. Many colleagues and graduate students have provided invaluable support for this project and for other endeavors in which I was simultaneously engaged. They read drafts, listened to ideas, helped track down sources, and organized bibliographies. I am likewise grateful for colleagues and graduate students who helped me make space for writing time in the face of numerous competing demands. Among them, I especially thank Phillip Tran, Susan Gardner, Sue Estler, Mary Madden, Elizabeth Barry, Lauri Sidelko, Andrea McGill-O'Rourke, Katie Jennings, Michelle Gayne, Susan Iverson, Suzanne Gordon, Lisa Hallen, Pamela Eddy, Jo-Ellen Carr, Jan Kristo, and Anne Pooler. Much appreciation is extended to my editors, Kelly Ward and Lisa Wolf-Wendel, for their patience, flexibility, and persistence. My sincere thanks to all the feminist scholars and practitioners whose work is central to this volume and who have contributed much to advancing women's status in higher education. Among them, Mary Ann Danowitz Sagaria, Patti Lather, Mary Margaret Fonow, Nancy Campbell, Judy Glazer-Raymo, Rebecca Ropers-Huilman, Sally Kitch, and Ann Schonberger have been instrumental in shaping my scholarship and nurturing my teaching in women's studies and feminist theory.

Published online in Wiley Online Library
(wileyonlinelibrary.com) • DOI: 10.1002/aehe.3701

Women's Status in Higher Education: Background and Significance

POLICY INITIATIVES, CURRICULAR REFORM, RESEARCH, and grassroots organizing have all contributed to advancing equity and shaping women's status in U.S. higher education. Nearly four or more decades have passed since key legislation, including the Equal Pay Act, Title VII, and Title IX, was passed and efforts were begun to broaden and create more inclusive curricula. Significant gains have been made in women's access to and representation in higher education as evidenced by enrollment figures and graduation rates. Yet these measures are only part of the full gender equity picture. For instance, when taken in the aggregate, enrollment data do not portray the persistent lack of gender parity among students studying engineering, computer science, and other science and technology fields, nor do they depict the quality of classroom and campus experiences. Even today, data reveal that women studying and working in postsecondary institutions bump up against glass ceilings and sticky floors, experience pay disparities linked to gender, and experience the threat and reality of sexual harassment and violence on campus.

Since 1988 more than half of all undergraduate students have been women, and 60 percent of students in graduate and professional programs in 2007–08 were women (King, 2010). These improvements in women's access to and representation in higher education are indeed impressive and worthy of note. Headlines based on these data alone, however—that is, drawing conclusions that equity has been achieved based on the overall proportion of faculty or students who are female—fail to acknowledge ways in which gender representation tends to be stratified across types of institutions and by rank

Women's Status in Higher Education　　　　　　　　　　　　　1

and discipline in institutions where women are underrepresented in particular fields, in the ranks of senior faculty in a majority of disciplines, and in senior leadership positions (King, 2010; Touchton, Musil, and Campbell, 2008).

A saying, *the higher the fewer*, continues to convey the current status of women in U.S. higher education as a result of their uneven representation among upper levels of prestige hierarchies in and between postsecondary institutions (Nidiffer, 2002). For instance, the figures pointing to the overall majority of women in graduate programs do not convey that male students remain the majority in both Ph.D. and M.D. programs (King, 2010), nor do they convey that women are more likely to be represented among faculty and leadership of community colleges and comprehensive four-year institutions than they are among the faculty and leadership share of elite research universities. Further, regardless of institutional type, women continue to hold fewer full professor positions than assistant professor and lecturer posts (Touchton, Musil and Campbell, 2008), and only 41 percent of women faculty were tenured compared with 55 percent of their male colleagues (Snyder, Dillow, and Hoffman, 2008). Female academic administrators are more likely to be located in female-dominated disciplines with lower status and lower salaries. In fact, community colleges are the only arena where women have attained parity (52 percent) as senior administrators. At research universities, women hold only 34 percent of senior administrative posts (King and Gomez, 2008).

Further, the numbers alone (whether aggregated or disaggregated) do not convey how women continue to report working and studying in climates that privilege masculine perspectives and approaches to organizing and leading that tend to disadvantage women (Martínez Alemán, 2008; Bornstein, 2008; Cooper and Stevens, 2002; Eddy and Cox, 2008; Glazer-Raymo, 2008a; Mason, Goulden, and Frasch, 2009; Sandler, Silverberg, and Hall, 1996; Valian, 1999). Climate-related issues like these along with complexities associated with demographic differences like race, sexual identity, and socioeconomic status among women all contribute to shaping women's experiences in higher education and therefore should be considered when assessing progress toward gender equity.

Guiding Assumptions and Questions

This monograph emerges from the premise that discrimination on the basis of one's sex, gender, race, socioeconomic status, sexual orientation, disability, religion, or ethnicity is harmful to advancing a civil society where all citizens have opportunities to contribute to their fullest potential. As microcosms of society, postsecondary institutions reflect, resist, and contribute to shaping norms of the larger culture in which they are situated. Lack of equity in higher education can have far-reaching and negative consequences for learning environments, quality of life, and career satisfaction of both women and men studying and working in academic institutions. Further, changes made (or not made) to promote equity in higher education can be of consequence beyond colleges and universities as administrators, faculty, and staff support and guide more than 19 million students (in the United States alone), produce knowledge that shapes culture, and engage in service to communities (Ropers-Huilman, 2003a; Snyder and Dillow, 2010).

Understanding social forces that have shaped and continue to shape understandings of culture can sharpen the lenses through which we examine the status of women in higher education and the status of other historically underrepresented groups. Moreover, these lenses can help illuminate complexities and avoid common pitfalls of framing gender equity in overly simplistic ways. For instance, when "women's status" is employed as a concept, it risks being understood in reductionist ways that fail to acknowledge differences among women. In turn, such conceptualizations allow "status" to be defined by issues most salient to white and economically privileged women, who have historically had the most access to the positional power and other privileges needed to shape gender equity agendas in higher education. Working to avoid such pitfalls is an important responsibility for those engaging in this and other conversations about women's status.

My focus on "women's status" in higher education is intended to foreground shared challenges women have faced and continue to face in patriarchal contexts while also acknowledging how race, social class, and other aspects of identity intersect with sex and gender and contribute to shaping one's professional status in profound ways. The purpose of this monograph is to provide a concise review of the contemporary status of women in U.S. higher education, including gains made and continuing challenges across diverse groups of women, and to delineate multiple lenses through which to understand and analyze persistent equity problems and strategies to address them. Toward that end, the following key questions are addressed in this and subsequent chapters:

What is the current status of women as students, faculty, and staff in U.S. higher education, including gains made in access, representation, and campus climate?

What are the persistent problems and challenges facing women working and studying in U.S. postsecondary institutions, including those producing disciplinary and occupational segregation?

What salient concepts have been proposed to promote understandings of gender equity?

How do demographic differences among women such as race, sexual identity, disability, age, and socioeconomic status contribute to shaping women's status?

What is feminist theory and how might its diverse frames be particularly helpful in analyzing the complexities of gender equity?

In light of these theoretical frameworks, what are some promising strategies for promoting gender equity in postsecondary institutions?

Responses to these questions provide a focus for both reviewing the literature about women's status in higher education and examining this status and its complexities through the lens of theory.

Historical Context

The status of women in higher education today is a product of its historical context and the confluence of numerous social and political forces. A number of scholars have expertly delineated histories of women in higher education (see, for example, Chamberlain, 1988; Nidiffer, 2000, 2002, 2010; Solomon, 1985). Drawing from these scholars and others who have described aspects of women's participation in U.S. postsecondary education, this chapter proceeds with a brief overview of the context from which our current conditions emerge. This historical context provides an important backdrop for understanding the gains made and continuing challenges for women in higher education today.

According to Nidiffer (2002), the realities for women in U.S. postsecondary education today are "the direct legacy of America's historical antagonism toward women's higher learning" (p. 3). The longstanding resistance to girls' and women's equal participation in schools and postsecondary institutions is evidence of this antagonism. Such resistance can be traced over centuries. At its inception, the purpose of American higher education, with the founding of Harvard College in 1636, was to prepare young men to become ministers and government leaders. Because society did not view women as suitable to such roles and girls lacked access to collegiate preparatory schools, women were also not considered as potential students in the colonial and most antebellum colleges.

Numerous sociopolitical events and related policy initiatives influenced social acceptance of women's participation in higher education in the decades following the Civil War. For example, more than seventy years of activism (from the Declaration of Sentiments and Resolutions presented at the Seneca Falls Convention in 1848 catalyzing the Suffrage Movement for women to the passage of the Nineteenth Amendment in 1920) helped to slowly shift the tide toward increasing public acceptance of women's participation in the civic realm. In addition, the Morrill Act of 1862 broadened public higher education and gradually, as coeducation expanded, provided more options for women seeking postsecondary training. By 1910 women represented 35 percent of all college students and were gaining entry into professional and graduate schools. These gains served to challenge longstanding cultural attitudes about women and often fueled backlash because of the perceived threat to male economic advantage (Nidiffer, 2001; Solomon, 1985). Thus, women's participation in higher education over the twentieth century ebbed and flowed. In the 1920s nearly half (47 percent) of college students were female, compared with only 30 percent from 1930 to 1950.

My research on university women's commissions provides a glimpse of how complex social forces contributed to shaping the status of women in U.S. society and in higher education during the ensuing decades of the 1960s and 1970s. Since their inception in 1968, university women's commissions have served to document the status, conditions, and positions of women and to recommend policy. The emergence of university women's commissions in the United States followed a pattern of women's commission development that can be traced to the international level with the formation of the United Nations Commission on the Status of Women in 1946. Initially, the primary role of the U.N. commission was to collect information and make recommendations related to women's rights globally. In the early 1960s, the U.N. commission undertook the task of promoting national women's commissions. By 1979 sixty-seven countries reported having some kind of women's commission or government division charged with similar functions (Stewart, 1980).

In the United States, the development of women's commissions stemmed from the first Presidential Commission on the Status of Women established in 1961 by executive order of President John F. Kennedy. The creation of this commission helped serve a number of political interests; it rewarded the many women who had supported Kennedy's campaign while maintaining their support for the next election. Ironically, the creation of this commission was also a means by which the Kennedy administration could deflect support for the Equal Rights Amendment (ERA). Kennedy was indebted to labor interests for his success in the presidential election the previous year, a constituency that strongly opposed the passage of the ERA (Stewart, 1980).

In light of this backdrop, it is not surprising that after twenty-two months of study, the Kennedy administration's Presidential Commission on the Status of Women produced a report concluding that the ERA was unnecessary. Despite this position, however, "the facts, in large part, spoke for themselves and called attention to the unfavorable condition of women in American society" (Stewart, 1980, p.7). The commission report generated institutional spin-offs, including the establishment of forty-five statewide commissions on the status of women within three years. Subsequent administrations followed Kennedy's lead and also appointed commission-like groups that advocated for women's policy concerns, including action on the ERA, enactment, and enforcement of antidiscrimination legislation, and support for new policies related to employment, education, childcare, women's health, pay equity, housing, and sexual harassment (Stewart, 1980). Although commissions were met with open hostility at times, it seemed their reports were most often marginalized or completely neglected by the administrations commissioning them (Rosenberg, 1982).

Catalyzed by the Presidential Commission on the Status of Women, women's state and local commissions grew in the mid-1960s and proliferated in the 1970s when the Women's Bureau in the Department of Labor supported their state-level establishment throughout the U.S. (Stewart, 1980). Although most of these commissions elected to pursue less contentious matters such as supporting educational functions by sponsoring conferences, developing newsletters, and holding hearings; a number of them also served in lobbying and administrative oversight capacities (Rosenberg, 1982). State and local commissions also performed the vital role of establishing networks among women—a condition that was integral to the growth of the women's movement. By 1980 local commissions existed in 150 communities in the United States (Stewart, 1980).

The earliest university women's commissions were formed in 1968 at the University of California, Berkeley, and the University of Chicago (Freeman, 1973). Although they were not limited to research universities, these institutions in particular initiated commissions on the status of women as a means of responding to demands made by women and to "demonstrate their good faith efforts" toward enhancing the status of women on campus (Glazer-Raymo, 1999, p. 66). Commissions were part of a growing number of women-focused higher education groups, including undergraduate and graduate women's caucuses, consciousness-raising groups, and academic discipline–related groups for women such as Committee W of the American Association of University Professors (Rossi and Calderwood, 1973).

Legislative and Policy Initiatives

A number of policy initiatives marked changes in societal dispositions and support for women's participation in higher education during the latter part of the twentieth century. For example, the Equal Pay Act mandating equal pay for equal work regardless of sex was passed in 1963, and Title VII of the 1964 Civil

Rights Act was amended to prohibit employment discrimination on the basis of sex. These landmark policies represented major legislative gains in the pursuit of equity. For women, however, the most vital policy instrument to mediate women's relationship with higher education was the passage of Title IX of the Education Amendments of 1972 (renamed the Patsy T. Mink Equal Opportunity in Education Act in 2002) prohibiting discrimination based on sex in educational programs receiving federal funds and requiring institutional audits.

Title IX emerged from efforts of the Women's Equity Action League, the National Organization for Women, legislators, and academic women throughout the United States whose focused activism was catalyzed by a class action suit filed by Bernice Sandler in 1969 and charging colleges and universities receiving federal funds with gender discrimination. The complaint prompted an outpouring of information and support from women in academia and women's rights groups in general.

Specifically, Title IX provides that "no person in the United States shall, on the basis of sex, be excluded from participation in, be denied the benefits of, or be subjected to discrimination under any education program or activity receiving Federal financial assistance" (Section 1681(a)). Although contemporary media attention to Title IX is most often associated with athletics, its coverage is much more expansive and includes such key issues as employment equity, sexual harassment, admissions, scholarships, pregnancy, and athletics (Somers, 2002).

Women in the Curriculum

Alongside the broader legislative context in the 1960s and 1970s, the academy was undergoing important changes from within that would shape the status of women in higher education in the years following. In particular, women students and faculty who had been involved with the civil rights and antiwar movements were calling societal power dynamics into question and challenging authority of commonly held perceptions of what counted as "truth" or legitimate knowledge. In the process, the exclusion and marginalization of women's contributions to society in textbooks and curricular materials were also coming under scrutiny. In response, women's studies courses were established in some colleges and universities and, in others, efforts were made to work toward more gender balance in existing courses. These initiatives were also accompanied and supported by the generation and growth of campus women's centers and centers for research on women (Schonberger, 2002).

Nevertheless, dispositional discrimination against women students, often reinforced by women themselves, has posed an ongoing challenge, even after the implementation of nondiscrimination or equity-enhancing policies and efforts to develop more inclusive curricula and pedagogies (Conway, Ahern, and Steuernagel, 1999). So while the numbers of women attending college and the numbers of women administrators have dramatically increased over the last three decades, "optimism in this regard should be tempered by the realization that before the passage of Title IX, the numbers of women in these positions was abysmally low" (Conway, Ahern, and Steuernagel, 1999, p. 24). As described previously, a cursory examination of the total percentages does not depict the nuances of the inequitable representation of women at upper levels of various prestige hierarchies in U.S. higher education. Further, researchers continue to find evidence of campus climates where the privileging of masculine perspectives and norms shapes and sustains inequitable experiences for women, including wage disparities (King, 2010); disproportionate representation of women as victims of relationship violence and sexual harassment (McMahon, 2008; Fisher, Cullen, and Turner, 2000; Hill and Silva, 2005); and attitudes toward work and family life, household responsibilities, and emotional labor that affect professional advancement for women (V. J. Rosser, 2004; Stout, Staiger, and Jennings, 2007).

Scholarship

Since the 1970s women's movement, scholarship by and about women has experienced unprecedented growth. Scholars from a range of fields have documented and produced knowledge about women's contributions to society and their development, health, and status in particular social arenas, including higher education. These scholars are far too numerous to be noted individually here, but their contributions have laid a strong foundation for many scholarly works referenced in this monograph. The literature specific to women in higher education emerged from the work of feminist academics from a range of disciplines committed to improving the experiences of women in colleges and universities. Pioneering scholars who applied feminist perspectives specifically to the study of higher education examined a range of topics, including access to higher education, student experiences and campus climate, the advancement of women employed in higher education, research and knowledge production, curricular issues, policy, leadership, and the organization of higher education (Aisenberg and Harrington, 1988; Chamberlain, 1988; Rossi and Calderwood, 1973).

In recent years, several scholarly volumes have been particularly noteworthy in drawing attention to the study of women in higher education, delineating key gender equity problems, offering perspectives for understanding, and proposing responses to those problems. *Women in Higher Education: A Feminist Perspective* (Glazer-Raymo, Townsend, and Ropers-Huilman, 2000) provided comprehensive approaches to the topic featuring essays and research summaries authored by feminist scholars from a range of disciplinary perspectives. In response to the breadth and depth several decades of research have produced, editors Martínez Alemán and Renn and contributors produced the encyclopedia *Women in Higher Education* (2002), with more than 120 academic contributors providing concise summaries of diverse topics in nine major content sections, for example: women in the curriculum, women and higher education policy, women students, staff, administrators, and employees. Glazer-Raymo's work in *Shattering the Myths: Women in Academe* (1999) and her edited volume *Unfinished Agendas: New and Continuing Gender Challenges in Higher Education* (2008b) examine in depth the sociopolitical and policy contexts shaping the status of women in higher education.

In 2008 the Project on the Status and Education of Women (initiated by Bernice Sandler in 1970) at the Association of American Colleges and Universities (AACU) published *A Measure of Equity: Women's Progress in Higher Education*. This thirty-seven-page data-driven report (Touchton, Musil, and Campbell, 2008) provides a concise synthesis of women's advancement toward full inclusion in the academy, documenting progress over four decades but also noting how the data reveal "the many areas where progress has been stymied or skewed by misinterpreted evidence" (p. v). Jacqueline King, from the American

Council on Education's (ACE's) Center for Policy Analysis, has produced several data-driven reports synthesizing national data and tracking progress relative to gender equity in higher education over time (King, 2000, 2006, 2010). And in 2007 Sue Klein of the Feminist Majority Foundation and more than two hundred contributors authored the *Handbook for Achieving Gender Equity Through Education,* which includes a summary of scholarship related to gender equity in postsecondary education at the turn of the twenty-first century (Cooper and others, 2007).

Offering a specific focus on how social constructions of gender shape higher education, authors contributing to Ropers-Huilman's edited volume *Gendered Futures in Higher Education: Critical Perspectives for Change* (2003b) examine ways in which higher education environments are deeply and problematically gendered. Issues specific to women and minority faculty are explored in *Tenure in the Sacred Grove* (Cooper and Stevens, 2002). Expanding the context and providing an explicit focus on theories of change, Sagaria and contributors offer international perspectives in *Women, Universities and Change: Gender Equality in the European Union and the United States* (2007b). In addition to the scholars who compiled these volumes, others—too numerous to mention by name here—have produced noteworthy scholarship about particular issues or approaches relevant to women in higher education. The work of many of them is included in this monograph.

In sum, the research produced about women in higher education and about gender equity in higher education is considerable. Nevertheless, persistent problems and gender-related challenges for women demonstrate the need for continued understanding and analysis. The depth and sophistication of the research have evolved; however, the body of work is relatively nascent and ripe for further exploration to help tease out, with more precision, the factors and complex dynamics that shape and enhance gender equity in the context of higher education. Although recent volumes and reports have examined the status of women in higher education from a feminist perspective, this monograph differs in that it describes a taxonomy for organizing the scholarship about women's status in higher education, and it highlights multiple and diverse theoretical frames for analyzing this scholarship and its applications.

Organization of this Monograph

The chapters included in this monograph are intended to both review the current scholarship about women's status in higher education and provide readers with multiple lenses through which to make meaning of that scholarship and its implications for changing the status quo. The following chapter delineates diverse feminist theories as frames for understanding equity and analyzing strategies to advance women's status. Although feminist theory is often employed in research related to gender equity and the status of women, it is less common for scholars to articulate the importance of differing (and often competing) assumptions shaping various conceptual approaches in feminism. As a result, readers of these works, especially those who have not studied feminist theory, might understandably assume the word "feminism" implies one particular view. Although feminisms share certain premises, they also differ in important ways, which can have profound implications for the ways in which problems are analyzed. Thus, scholars and practitioners stand to gain new analytic tools by developing more nuanced understandings of feminist theory. Most important, expanding or refining lenses for analyzing persistent equity problems will also help expand the potential for resolving them.

The following two chapters, "Examining Women's Status: Access and Representation as Key Equity Indicators" and "Examining Women's Status: Campus Climate and Gender Equity," provide an overview of the current literature about gender equity in higher education. This review of the scholarship could have been organized chronologically by tracing developments over time or by constituent groups such as women students, staff, and faculty. Instead, I chose to organize the scholarship according to its primary emphasis on describing status in terms of access and representation or climate-related issues. These entities are not necessarily discrete, as many studies consider both representation and climate, but in the end, most scholarship tends to emphasize one over the other. Thus, this approach provided the most flexible framework for organizing and examining multiple dimensions and indicators of gender equity described in the literature.

The focus in the third chapter is access and representation; "access" is defined in terms of gatekeeping (gaining entry to institutions of higher education), and "representation" refers to *where* women are located or positioned once they have gained access to the institution as students, faculty, staff, or administrators. The chapter takes a closer look at the phenomenon of "the higher the fewer" for women in terms of their representation relative to occupational segregation and prestige hierarchies in and across institutions. Representation also refers to gaining access to particular institutional arenas like athletics, science, technology, engineering, and mathematics (STEM) fields, senior leadership roles, and senior faculty as well as the representation of women in different types of postsecondary institutions.

The following chapter shifts from describing numbers and locations of women in various higher education arenas to describing the experiences of women in different roles and contexts within postsecondary institutions. This emphasis is captured by the word "climate"—generally defined as "common member perceptions, assumptions, beliefs, feelings or attitudes" about organizational life (Cress, 2002, p. 391). Building on Peterson and Spencer's overview (1990), Cress (2002) describes key characteristics that distinguish the concepts of campus culture and climate. Although these terms are often used interchangeably, they are distinct. Campus culture, typically conceptualized from anthropological and sociological perspectives, refers to values deeply embedded in the organizational structure and is therefore considered enduring in nature. In contrast, the concept of campus climate emerges from conceptual frameworks of cognitive and social linguistics, psychology, and organizational behavior and emphasizes more current patterns of behavior and perceptions of an organization, which tend to be more malleable or susceptible to change (Cress, 2002; Hart and Fellabaum, 2008).

The following chapter, "Advancing Women's Status: Analyzing Predominant Strategies" shines the spotlight on change making by providing a review of the literature related to predominant strategies for advancing gender equity in the context of higher education. Many of these strategies such as policy initiatives are not limited to higher education but are included because they have had profound effects on women's status in higher education. The strategies are organized by theme and include reviews of literature related to activism, organizing, and women's networks; policy-focused strategies; mentoring; augmenting institutional infrastructures; leadership development; altering organizational norms and practices; and curriculum transformation, including women's studies, feminist epistemology, and women-focused research centers. Building on the conceptual framing provided earlier, the chapter examines strategies through multiple lenses of feminist theory to help make embedded assumptions more explicit and examine ways in which these assumptions serve to shape and constrain the range of possible solutions to the problem of inequity.

The final chapter includes recommendations for further research and a brief discussion of the implications of drawing on multiple lenses to analyze equity. Several questions help guide the summary and set the stage for further exploration:

Based on the extant scholarship, what conclusions can be drawn about the current status of women in higher education?

What issues need further exploration?

Based on the literature, what assertions can be made about strategies to advance the status of women in higher education?

When considering strategies to advance gender equity in higher education, what feminist perspectives are most and least represented?

What are the underlying assumptions framing the problem-solving approaches, and what are their potential implications?

What recommendations can be offered based on this analysis?

Framing Women's Status Through Multiple Lenses

A S PREVIOUSLY SET FORTH, substantial gains have been made along the path toward equity, yet persistent problems remain and some areas show evidence of regression (Glazer-Raymo, 2008a, 2008b). These findings prompt questions about types of strategies best suited to securing advances made and potentially increasing the pace with which we are able to close remaining equity gaps. Although these questions are certainly not new, I am suggesting that there are *different ways* in which the same questions can be framed and that the process of reframing may lead to a wider range of potential solutions.

This chapter proceeds from the premise that approaches to achieving equity emerge from particular perspectives about the nature of the problem(s) of inequity. If some perspectives are overlooked in the process of identifying and understanding the problem of inequity, then it is reasonable to assume potential strategies for solving the problem will also be overlooked. Considering the intractability of some equity problems, it seems vital to take a step back and examine underlying assumptions about ways in which the problems are framed.

Some research suggests that even the most well-intentioned approaches to gender equity tend to frame the problems through a dominant lens and may undercut their desired goals (Allan, 2008; Allan, Iverson, and Ropers-Huilman, 2010; Bacchi, 1999; De Castell and Bryson, 1997). This approach is difficult to avoid because such lenses are dominant and are rarely called into question. This chapter exposes dominant lenses, not because they are necessarily unproductive but because they may be limited in their usefulness and because they eclipse other potentially promising ways of analyzing and resolving inequity.

Why Theory?

In general, theory is a research-based explanatory framework or guide that can help us make sense of our experiences and the complexity of the world in which we live. As Bunch and Pollack (1983) explained, "The purpose of theory is not to provide a pat set of answers about what to do, but to guide us in sorting out options and keep us aware of the questions that need to asked" (p. 13). Frequently, theory and practice are described in ways that emphasize their distinctions. This conceptualization (between those who theorize and those who "do things") reinforces the notion that theory is something separate and distinct from the mundane or material aspects of daily life. As Bunch and Pollack (1983) reminded us, however, "The question is not whether we have a theory, but how aware we are of the assumptions behind our actions and how conscious we are of the daily choices we make among different theories" (p. 13). For example, when those working toward gender equity in higher education choose to put energy into building a women's center or hiring more women in leadership roles, they are acting according to certain theories about power and how to best advance change in light of these assumptions.

Applying theory as a lens through which to view the social world is a powerful analytic process with significant implications for social change. Viewing problems from multiple angles or through multiple lenses can help illuminate different aspects of the problem and therefore shift or broaden the manner in which we choose to resolve it. For instance, "safety" is commonly considered a problem for women on college campuses. Over the years, numerous strategies have been implemented to address this identified problem, including improved campus lighting, self-defense classes, escort services, and wallet cards with phone numbers of campus police. Although such efforts are well meaning and may be helpful, a closer look reveals that these predominant approaches are designed primarily to help alleviate women's fear but do not address the root cause of the fear—men's violence or constructions of aggressive masculinity that normalize men's violence (Allan, 2003, 2008). In this case, it is easy to see how applying a different lens illuminates potential short-comings of dominant approaches to framing problems and solutions related to campus safety; as well, reframing the problem from a new angle opens up the potential for different and more effective change strategies.

As the previous chapter delineated, scholars have adopted a range of approaches to analyzing gender-based inequity in higher education. For example, Sagaria's edited collection (2007a, 2007b) is framed by theories of organizational change and, more specifically, the lens of organizational adaptation to understand how higher education's responses to sociopolitical and economic influences affect gender equality in both the European Union and the United States. Another example is Valian's text *Why So Slow? The Advancement of Women* (1999), which includes a chapter focused on women in academia. In this text, Valian draws specifically from social psychological theories and applies the conceptual lens of gender schemas to explain how "a set of implicit, or nonconscious, hypotheses about sex differences plays a central role in shaping men's and women's professional lives" (p. 2). These and other analyses of women's status in higher education are either implicitly or explicitly feminist in their approach (see Glazer-Raymo, 1999, 2008b; Glazer-Raymo, Townsend, and Ropers-Huilman, 2000). Each of them—and others as well—provides approaches and perspectives important to furthering understanding about gender equity and the status of women in higher education. This monograph builds on and supplements the work of these scholars by examining gender equity in higher education through multiple feminist frames.

Why *Feminist* Theory?

Feminist theories are particularly suited to the examination of gender equity because they encompass a range of approaches to the problems of discrimination and oppression (Reinharz, 1992). Sharing in their acknowledgment of gender-based inequalities in society, feminist theories can help us see connections among parts of one's life that have not previously been seen and help us think about criteria for change (Lugones and Spelman, 1983). Over the last four decades, feminism has evolved to encompass theorizing that acknowledges the fluidity of women's multiple identities, including intersections of race, social class, citizenship, sexual identity, and disability. Other theoretical approaches share in feminist goals of analyzing discriminatory practices and promoting more egalitarian social relations, including critical theory and post-colonial theory. A *feminist* approach to inquiry, however, more specifically describes research that seeks social change while also emphasizing women and gender as key analytic categories. I align most closely with feminist approaches that foreground intersections of gender and sex with other salient aspects of sociocultural identity (for example, Lugones, 2003; Mohanty, 1991; Weedon, 1999).

Stereotypes often shape perceptions and misunderstandings about feminism. Media images of feminists as man haters or "femi-Nazis" tend to gain currency when the status quo is challenged and political backlash ensues. Given this scenario, accurate information about feminism is a crucial starting point. I have found that many students in my undergraduate and graduate courses are surprised to learn that not all feminists share like-minded views about the nature of gender and oppression. Although important distinctions exist among feminist approaches to resolving problems of inequity rooted in gender and sociocultural identity differences, vital commonalities are also obvious: (1) sex and gender inequality exists and is central to social relations and the structuring of social institutions; (2) sex and gender inequality is not "natural" or essential but a product of social relations; and (3) sex and gender inequality should be eliminated through social change. I often encounter individuals who find they agree with these premises yet had not previously considered themselves feminists.

Although shared premises provide an important starting point for understanding feminist theory, it is equally important to understand that feminism is not a singular perspective or ideology. In approaching the range of feminist theories, Tong (2009) explains, "Feminist thought is old enough to have a history complete with a set of labels" (p. 1). This range of labels reflects key distinctions among feminist perspectives about the nature of power, oppression, and approaches to change. Interdisciplinary and wide ranging in their analytic applications, feminist theories are complex and nuanced. Although labels are reductive and can fail to reflect many of the complexities in and between them, they can also help, at least provisionally, signify the range of perspectives feminists have drawn on to explain women's oppression and propose solutions for its elimination (Tong, 2009).

An in-depth treatment of each feminist frame is beyond the scope of this monograph but is the subject of numerous texts, including, for instance, Kolmar and Bartkowski (2010), McCann and Kim (2003), and Tong (2009). My purpose in this chapter, however, is to provide a general overview primarily for those new to the subject of feminist theory. In so doing, I hope to contribute to shaping lenses for understanding the framing of "women's issues" and "gender in/equity" and in turn expand the range of possible approaches to improving women's status.

Multiple Frames

The following overview of theoretical frameworks common to feminist thought includes descriptions of liberal, radical, socialist, multicultural (global) and postcolonial, ecofeminist, psychological, poststructural or postmodern, and third-wave feminist thought. The frameworks might be variously characterized as labels, strands of feminist theory, or schools of thought. Whatever the terminology employed, these labels signal that feminist theory is not a monolithic ideology. And although the labels are "incomplete and highly contestable, they remain serviceable" as a reminder that feminist theory is diverse in its explanations of and proposed solutions for inequity (Tong, 2009, p. 1).

The review of each school of thought provides a snapshot of its key characteristics and highlights some of the prominent scholars noted as advancing theories from that particular perspective. Additionally, they draw on Allen's work (1999, 2005) for delineating the predominant ways in which power has been conceptualized in feminism and feminist theory: (1) power as a resource to be redistributed, (2) power as domination (oppression, patriarchy) or "power-over," and (3) individual and collective empowerment or "power-to" act. According to Allen (2005), most feminist literature has evolved around a view of power as domination (patriarchy) and how women can be liberated from this source of oppression. Some feminist theories, however, have emerged by reconceptualizing power and focusing more on power as an ability or capacity to act in ways that enhance (or produce) rather than power as the capacity to erode (or repress) others (Allen, 1999, 2005). Each of these versions of power is described in the following sections, beginning with the view of power as a resource to be shared equally—a cornerstone of the liberal feminist tradition.

Liberal Feminism

The perspective informing the vast majority of gender equity initiatives in education and policy arenas is liberal feminism, or what is sometimes referred to as "enlightenment liberal feminism" (Donovan, 1993). This school of thought emerged from political theories of classical and welfare liberalism with their emphasis on rationality and reason as unique qualities of human beings. Liberal feminists contend discrimination against women is fundamentally unfair and not in keeping with a just society's need to foster human rights and the ability for individuals to exercise autonomy and self-fulfillment (Tong, 2009). In general, the focus of liberal feminism is rights, justice, and fairness as key concepts for eliminating gender-based discrimination. Because most contemporary feminist theory defines itself in relation to liberal feminism, a basic understanding of this school of thought can serve as a helpful starting point (Tong, 2009).

Liberal feminist perspectives are framed by understandings of power as a positive social good—a good that is distributed unequally on the basis of sex or gender (and other identity formations in more recent versions of liberal feminism). Thus, in liberal feminism, power is conceptualized as a resource or something to be possessed. "For feminists who understand power in this way, the goal is to redistribute this resource so that women will have power equal to men" (Allen, 2005, p. 4).

The liberal approach to women's rights gained momentum from the eighteenth and nineteenth century writings of Mary Wollstonecraft, John Stuart Mill, and Harriet Taylor, who crafted arguments in favor of women's rights to education and influence in the public domain. Building on political thought of the time, Wollstonecraft argued in *Vindication of the Rights of Women* (Kolmar and Bartkowski, 2010) that women were just as capable of rational thought as men and thus, like men, deserved to become autonomous decision makers. Her vision of a "woman strong in mind and body, a person who is not a slave to her passions, her husband, or her children" (Tong, 2009, p. 15) was radical for the privileged classes of that time, who viewed ideal woman-hood as fragile, passive, emotional, and without capacity for reason (Kolmar and Bartkowski, 2010). Many others contributed to the developing focus on women's rights during and before this period, including, for example, Abigail Adams in colonial America with her admonishment that women have some "voice or representation" in the "new Code of Laws," and Olympe de Gouges, in France, who was guillotined after producing a street pamphlet "On the Equality of the Sexes" in 1791 (Donovan, 1993).

Building on Wollstonecraft's thesis, Sarah Grimké's *Letters on Equality* in 1838 presented "one of the most cogent and elegant arguments against women's subordination developed in the liberal tradition" (Donovan, 1993, p. 13). Likewise, Harriet Taylor (1851) asserted women could indeed be partners with men in life and work and not simply objects of beauty. Offering their perspectives as the Industrial Revolution unfolded, both Taylor and Mill emphasized women's economic potential. Mill in particular argued in *The Subjection of Women* (1870) that "if women's rational powers were recognized as equal to men's, then society would reap significant benefits" (Tong, 2009, p. 18). Both Mill and Taylor challenged societal assumptions about male superiority and women's place in the public realm while at the same time maintaining allegiance to the idea that women possessed unique maternal and care-giving roles in society. Wollstonecraft, Mill, and Taylor's contributions helped pave the way for arguments in favor of the vote for women in the United States and Britain (Kolmar and Bartkowski, 2010; Tong, 2009).

Since 1920 and the passage of suffrage for women in the United States, liberal feminist ideals have played a prominent role in women's movements and concomitant strategies in the United States and throughout the world. The focus on social reform, and ultimately the redistribution of power through suffrage, access to education, and implementation of laws and institutional policies, is evidenced, for example, in the twentieth-century writings of Betty Friedan, the work of the National Organization for Women, and the passage of laws such as Title IX that have helped advance equity for women by facilitating access to and expanded participation in postsecondary education. In the context of higher education in particular, commissions on the status of women, equal employment and opportunity offices, efforts to ensure equitable salaries, and efforts to increase the numbers of women in the pipeline reflect liberal feminist approaches to change.

Radical Feminism

Alternatively, radical feminists argue that reform-oriented approaches like those evolving from liberal feminism will never be sufficient to eliminate the oppression of women that is, in their view, rooted in patriarchal systems. Because educational institutions as well as the legal and institutional systems in which policies operate are supported by patriarchal systems, radical feminists argue that these vehicles cannot possibly undo the oppression of women. In other words, "The master's tools will never dismantle the master's house" (Lorde, 1984, p. 110).

Influenced by the revolutionary ideas and strategies of radical social reform movements during the civil rights and antiwar era, radical feminism moves away from approaches to change that operate within the established systems or through strategies that have emerged from those systems. Rather, radical feminists favor a complete overhaul, dismantling, or uprooting of patriarchy and its social and cultural institutions. As such, a radical feminist might argue that reform-oriented approaches like mentoring programs, professional development, or commissions on the status of women appointed by the government or institutions of higher education are not likely to produce enduring change because they fail to eradicate the root causes of inequity.

The radical feminist shift away from reform-oriented approaches of liberal feminism is supported by a shift in understandings of power and how power operates. In contrast to liberal feminism where power is understood as a resource in need of redistribution, radical feminism tends to view power in terms of dyadic models of dominance and subordination relationships (Allen, 2005).

Although radical feminism is most easily recognized by its skepticism of liberal feminism's approach to achieving gender equity by reforming male-dominated systems and institutions, a closer examination reveals a more complex theoretical landscape. To help sort out some of the nuances in this school of thought, Tong (2009) describes radical feminism as comprising of two basic groups—radical-libertarian and radical-cultural feminists. These labels reflect differences in how each conceptualizes root causes of sexism or patriarchy and its elimination.

Both strands of radical feminist thought share in their emphasis on the centrality of sex, gender, and reproduction as the means to achieve true liberation for women. Radical-libertarian feminists argue that the rigidity of socially constructed gender roles is harmful to both men and women and that liberation will result when these norms are transformed such that women and men are free to explore and choose both feminine and masculine dimensions and achieve a sense of wholeness. Alternatively, radical-cultural feminists question the turn toward androgyny as a viable liberation strategy for women. For instance, these feminists point out that the problem for women is not adherence to femininity but the devaluing of femininity that is most problematic. If women abandon femininity in favor of androgyny, might doing so lend more support for the dominance of masculinity within patriarchy? Similar differences also mark debates around the most prudent ways to conceptualize sex and reproduction such that transformative change and true liberation for women are more likely to occur. For instance, radical-liberation feminists argue that biological motherhood can drain women of physical and psychic energy and, as such, women should have control of their reproductive lives to both prevent and produce pregnancy with or without the involvement of men. Alternatively, radical-cultural feminists affirm women's biological motherhood as the ultimate source of female power and encourage cultural valuation of that power (Tong, 2009).

This brief overview provides only a glimpse of the assumptions that set radical feminism apart from liberal feminism. In building the case for more radical and transformative approaches to achieving equity and liberation for women, both radical-libertarian [such as Shulamith Firestone (1970), Gayle Rubin (1975), and Kate Millett (1969)] and radical-cultural [for example, Mary Daly (1978, 1984) and Marilyn French (1985)] feminists have made powerful contributions to feminist scholarship. Of the many topics explored and debated from radical feminist perspectives, some of the most prominent include relationships between patriarchy and gender roles, the sex/gender system (Rubin, 1975), sexual politics (Millett, 1969), power, reproduction, pornography, God, language, and sexual identities. In each of these areas, radical feminists both agree and disagree. So although radical feminists agree that the reform agenda of liberal feminism is insufficient to eliminate the oppression of women (and other forms of oppression as well), they do not always agree on how best to accomplish this goal.

Marxist, Socialist, and Materialist Feminism

Marxist, socialist, and materialist feminists argue that a class-based society is the underlying cause of oppression and emphasize the dismantling of capitalism as the key pathway to the liberation of women. Similarly, socialist feminists argue that capitalism and patriarchy are mutually reinforcing systems. Thus, socialist feminists contend both systems (patriarchy and capitalism) need to be dismantled for women to achieve equal standing with men (Tong, 2009). Like radical feminism, the view of power for Marxist and socialist feminist thinkers tends to be one of power-over, or power that supports systems of domination.

Marxist and socialist feminist approaches were initially catalyzed in the 1970s when feminist thinkers critiqued the gender-blind approach offered in Karl Marx's account of power as result of domination through class exploitation (Allen, 2005). Although Marx offered a compelling analysis of class exploitation through economic production, feminists pointed out that he overlooked "women's reproductive labor in the home and the exploitation of this labor in capitalist modes of production" (p. 10). Thus, feminist thinkers such as Eisenstein (1979) and Hartmann (1981) argued that Marx's analysis must be supplemented with a critique of patriarchy (Allen, 2005; Tong, 2009).

An early example of an application of a Marxist approach in feminist thought and activism was the wages-for-housework campaign of the 1970s, which was based on the reasoning that women's work in the private sphere (the home) is a necessary condition for all labor and that "by providing not only food and clothes but also emotional comfort to current (and future) workers, women keep the cogs of the capitalist machine running" (Tong, 2009, p. 109). Recognizing that a socialist approach made sense theoretically but in practicality did not yield liberation for women in socialist systems, Marxist and socialist feminists turned to more nuanced explanations of women's oppression and, in turn, strategies for change. Thinkers such as Alison Jaggar

(1983), Iris Marion Young (1990), Heidi Hartmann (1981), and Sylvia Walby (1986) explored capitalism-patriarchal connections and focused on a range of topics, including women's labor issues, the gender wage gap, global markets, multinational corporations, and sweat shops.

An examination of the philosophical differences between thinkers who identify as materialist feminists rather than Marxist or socialist is beyond the scope of this monograph. Generally speaking, these strands tend to share some fundamental theoretical assumptions and goals that emphasize the centrality of capitalism and class issues. Materialist feminist approaches, however, also tend to emphasize the importance of ideologies of race, sexuality, imperialism, and colonialism (Landry and MacLean, 1993). An in-depth exploration of materialist feminism is provided in *Materialist Feminism and the Politics of Difference* (Hennessey, 1993) and *Materialist Feminism: A Reader in Class, Difference, and Women's Lives* (Hennessy and Ingraham, 1997).

Multicultural, Global, and Postcolonial Feminism

Despite support for the analytic lenses offered by liberal, radical, Marxist, and socialist perspectives, multicultural and global or postcolonial feminists argue these frameworks often fail to acknowledge important differences in the category "women," and in the process, they tend to highlight perspectives of privileged white women. Although differences exist, multicultural, global, and postcolonial feminism share in the foregrounding of diversity among women and in acknowledging the challenges it represents in feminist activism and theory. Views of power in multicultural, global, and postcolonial strands of feminist thought vary and can include conceptualizations of power as a resource, power as domination, and power as empowerment, depending on the particular perspective.

Some differentiate multicultural feminists from global or postcolonial feminists by reserving the word "multicultural" to "denote feminists who focus on the differences that exist among women who live within the boundaries of one nation-state or geographical area" (Tong, 2009, p. 8). Building on and expanding multicultural feminist perspectives, global and postcolonial feminists emphasize interconnections among women throughout the world but also draw attention to the ways in which gains for women in so-called developed nations like the United States are often made at the expense of the well-being of women in so-called developing nations and areas (Enloe, 1990; Mohanty, 1991, 2003; Narayan, 1997). According to Bunch (1987), "The oppression of women in one part of the world is often affected by what happens in another, and . . . no woman is free until the conditions of oppression of women are eliminated everywhere" (p. 301).

Importantly, multicultural, global, and postcolonial approaches argue that other differences, including sexual identity and orientation, physical ability, social class, religion, and age, are also aspects of identity that can affect women's experiences of discrimination and that the definition of feminism should therefore be expanded to include all social systems that oppress women. For instance, global and postcolonial feminists have asserted that perspectives emerging from so-called First World feminists often place priority on sexuality and reproduction as key gender issues, while political and economic issues tend to be highlighted in so-called Third World perspectives (Tong, 2009).

Feminists debate the salience of particular aspects of identity in relation to experiences of oppression, resulting in a range of explanatory concepts such as "intersectionality" (Crenshaw, 1997) and "interlocking systems of domination" (Collins, 1991; Hooks, 1984) to denote the ways in which women across many different identity categories are different but also connected (Mohanty, 2003; Narayan, 1997). Patricia Hill Collins, Audre Lorde, Elizabeth Spelman, Charlotte Bunch, Bell Hooks, Maria Lugones, Chandra Mohanty, Alice Walker, Mitsuye Yamada, Kimberlé Crenshaw, Trinh Minh-ha, and Gloria Anzaldua are among numerous feminist thinkers shaping the debates from multicultural, global, and postcolonial perspectives. These debates are wide-ranging and include themes related to challenges of conceptualizing race and other sociocultural identity differences among women; relations between global markets, politics of development, and the status of women globally; sexual and reproductive issues such as the promotion of sterilization among particular populations, sex trafficking of girls and women, and the use of reproductive technologies for sex selection in favor of male fetuses; coalition building among diverse women, women's rights as human rights, and deconstructing imperialist assumptions embedded in approaches to research, knowledge production, and what counts as "truth."

Ecofeminism

Inclusive of, yet not limited to, analyses of capitalism; patriarchy; and socio-cultural differences among women, ecofeminist approaches offer broad-reaching perspectives. Ecofeminism differs from other strands in that it specifically high-lights how the oppression of women is inextricably tied to ways in which humans interact with each other and the nonhuman world. Although ecofeminists describe conditions of domination, they tend to place a greater empha-sis on empowerment (power-to) in their analyses and recommendations for change (Allen, 2005).

Drawing on the myriad of symbolic, conceptual, and linguistic evidence of the gendering of nature (for example, "mother nature"), ecofeminists argue that human domination over and desire to control nature is inextricably linked to male domination of women or patriarchy. King (1989) summarized this view when she stated: "We live in a culture that is founded on the repudiation and domination of nature. This has special significance for women because, in patriarchal thought, women are believed to be closer to nature than men. This gives women a particular stake in ending the domination of nature—in healing the alienation between human and nonhuman nature" (p. 470).

From an ecofeminist perspective, relationships of domination and subor-dination are central to analyzing women's status, and, thus, the transforma-tion of such relations is fundamental to advancing true liberation for women. Ecofeminists work to deconstruct prestige-based hierarchies not only among humans but also between humans and nature. As such, ecofeminism is char-acterized by analyses that foreground logics of domination employed to jus-tify subordination among humans and other living things. Different theorists tend to emphasize particular aspects of ecofeminism, resulting in diverse per-spectives within this frame. For example, some, like Mary Daly (1978), Sherry Ortner (1995), and Susan Griffin (1978), take different approaches but share in affirming the woman-nature connection. Others, like Starhawk (1979, 1989, 2002) and Carol Christ (2003) tend to emphasize spiritual perspectives strongly influenced by earth-centered theologies that honor women and nature as sacred. Others in ecofeminism, including Dorothy Dinnerstein (1989) and Karen J. Warren (2000), take a more social constructivist view alongside global perspectives like those of Maria Mies and Vandana Shiva (1993).

In their essay about ecofeminist visions for change, Mies and Shiva (1993) emphasize that transformation must be approached as both a material and spiritual endeavor. In so doing, they point to a number of strategies rooted in a subsistence lifestyle, for example, being conscious of producing only as much as one can use and consuming only as much as one needs to live. They also suggest replacing representative democracy with participatory government to ensure each individual has a voice; breaking down boundaries between work and play, sciences and arts, spirit and matter; and promoting traditionally feminine traits like caring, compassion, and nurturance for all people (pp. 318–322). A helpful source for a more in-depth examination of ecofeminist approaches is Warren's *Ecofeminist Philosophy: A Western Perspective on What It Is and Why It Matters* (2000).

Psychological Feminism

In contrast to the global and the broad ecological views of multicultural and ecofeminist perspectives are the psychoanalytic and psychological care-focused strands of feminism (for example, Carol Gilligan and Nel Noddings). Despite vast differences between them, I have grouped these frames together because they represent feminist theories that take an intrapersonal approach to examining women and women's experiences in the social world.

Psychoanalytic feminism is complex and nuanced, but generally speaking, feminists who theorize from this perspective "claim the roots of women's oppression are embedded deep in the female psyche" (Tong, 2009, p. 5). Although feminists like Betty Friedan and Shulamith Firestone have critiqued Freud's theories (and concepts like "penis envy") as misogynist, some feminists leave open the possibility that a version of Freud's Oedipus complex may be valid (Macdonald, 2002). Other feminists are considered psychoanalytic because they locate root causes of oppression in the unconscious. Still others have moved beyond Freud to theorize the pre-Oedipal or the prelinguistic realm of human development and understandings of subjectivity as a potential site of liberation for women (Tong, 2009). Some well-known feminist thinkers who are considered psychoanalytic in their approaches include Karen Horney, Clara Thompson, Dorothy Dinnerstein, Nancy Chodorow, Juliet Mitchell, Helene Cixous, Jane Flax, Teresa de Lauretis, and Diana Fuss.

The psychic realm of women has also been explored in other ways. For example, Gilligan (1982), Noddings (1989), and Belenky, Clinchy, Goldberger, and Tarule (1986) tend to focus less on Oedipal and sexuality-based reasons for women's oppression and liberation and emphasize the care-focused and relational aspects of women's cognition. Similar to the cultural strand of radical feminism described earlier, these approaches tend to highlight the feminine or female propensity for caring as a human strength (rather than liability) and emphasize caring, community, and connection as the preferred means of eliminating oppression of women. In this way, care-focused feminism, like ecofeminism, tends to highlight an empowerment (power-to) conceptualization of power.

Postmodern, Poststructural, and Third Wave Feminism

Postmodern and poststructural feminist thought is informed by postmodern and poststructural critiques of liberal humanist philosophy. More specifically, these approaches are characterized by critiques of humanist versions of personhood conceptualized as a rational, coherent, and essential self or subject. Postmodern and poststructural approaches also depart from conceptualizations of power as a limited-quantity resource to be possessed and instead emphasize power as something produced through language and representation. This view of power as productive rather than primarily repressive underpins the postmodern challenge to the concept of an essential or predetermined subject and replaces it with a more fluid view of subjectivity or a subject-in-process.

Poststructuralism does not carry a singular or fixed meaning yet the theories connected by this label contain a number of common premises. Among them is the premise that language and discourse not only reflect but also produce sociopolitical realities. This premise characterizes poststructuralist discourse theory, a term describing a group of theories largely influenced by the work of Foucault (1978, 1979) and other poststructural thinkers including Derrida, Kristeva, and Irigaray (Baxter, 2003).

Poststructuralism can be understood as an academic branch of postmodernism, where "postmodern" refers to larger cultural and philosophical shifts (reflected in art, architecture, politics, and new media, for example). Postmodern perspectives highlight a skepticism about universal causes, absolutes, and truths

(Lather, 1991, 1992; Baxter, 2003) that undergird modernist views of reality. In so doing, postmodern perspectives also challenge modernist visions of an autonomous and rational subject. In place of these universal truths and fixed identities, postmodernism posits a vision of reality and subjectivity that is dynamically constituted through discourse.

Against the backdrop of postmodernism, *poststructuralism* refers to a loosely connected group of theories predicated on a critique of structuralist approaches to the investigation of language. Structuralist approaches to linguistics proceed from the premise that language, as a meaning-making system, carries fixed or intrinsic ideas that provide an ultimate correspondence to the world (Scott, 1988) and could thus discern the true meaning of a text by analyzing its deep structures and author's motivations. In contrast, poststructuralist theories assert that language is socially constituted and shaped by the interplay among texts, readers, and the larger cultural context rather than carrying any kind of fixed or inherent meaning that can be "discovered." In sum, poststructuralism moves away from structural assumptions of essential and fixed meanings in language to provide an approach that views language or discourse as the "site for the construction and contestation of social meanings" (Baxter, 2003, p. 6).

Subjectivity constituted through discourse implies that each of us is continually engaged in a process of locating ourselves as we draw on discourses to represent ourselves. From this perspective, personhood or the self is not fixed, unified, or essential (determined in advance of discourse) as a modernist or liberal humanist view implies. Poststructuralism emphasizes dynamic, local, and productive properties of power, in contrast to limited supply and power as a resource concept that undergirds liberal feminism.

In sum, feminist postmodern and poststructuralist thought highlights multiplicity and fluidity of identities and the importance of productive power as it operates through dominant discourses to produce conditions where women's oppression is more likely to occur. Well-known and often-cited feminist poststructuralist thinkers such as Helene Cixous, Judith Butler, Chris Weedon, Sara Mills, Patti Lather, Wanda Pillow, Elizabeth St. Pierre, Rebecca Ropers-Huilman, and Estela Bensimon have advanced applications of feminist poststructuralism and its implications for teaching, research, and policy (Allan, Iverson, and Ropers-Huilman, 2010).

Third-wave feminism shares a number of similarities with feminist postmodern and poststructural perspectives but is also different in a number of respects. In many ways it is a hybrid of several feminist frames previously described. In terms of commonalities with other feminist frames, third-wave feminism is characterized by willingness to foreground diversity (similar to multicultural feminism) as well as change and ambiguity (similar to poststructural feminism). Third-wave feminists also share with poststructural and postmodern feminists the desire to disrupt binary oppositions through speaking and writing that deconstructs socially constituted dichotomies and phallocentrism (Tong, 2009).

Summary

The perspectives offered in each feminist frame provide insights for analyzing the complexities of oppression and for developing effective strategies to eliminate its associated problems and root causes. This overview of feminist schools of thought provides a snapshot of the diversity in the labels "feminism" and "feminist theory." From the reform-oriented approaches of liberal feminism and Marxist and socialist feminism to the more transformative approaches of radical feminism and ecofeminism, from the distinct perspectives of multicultural, global, postcolonial, and poststructural feminism to the intrapersonal approaches of psychoanalytic and care-focused feminism, feminist thought encompasses a myriad of perspectives that provide divergent views of systems and dynamics that sustain the oppression of women. Exhibit 1 summarizes key distinctions between different frames of feminist theory and makes some preliminary links between them and conceptualizations of inequity in the context of higher education.

Although this chapter highlighted particular labels in feminist theory, it would be a mistake to assume these labels always represent discrete categories. Some feminist thinkers position themselves in a particular school of thought, but it is not uncommon to find feminist thinkers who blur boundaries by working the interstices of two or more perspectives. In sum, feminist theory is not easily reduced to neat and tidy categories. For instance, some ecofeminist theories share in a global approach, and liberal feminism has increasingly offered more multicultural and global perspectives.

EXHIBIT 1

Feminist Frames, Power, and Change

Feminist Frame	Liberal	Radical	Socialist	Multicultural/ Global/ Post-colonial	Cofeminist	Psychological • psychoanalytic • care-focused	PM/poststrux Third Wave
Key Areas of Emphasis	Equality of opportunity	Male domination of women; patriarchy	Mutually reinforcing systems of capitalism and patriarchy	Cultural, economic, racial, national, differences among women; simultaneity of oppressions.	Logics of domination manifest in many forms, including human over nonhuman world	Intrapersonal psychic the unconscious pre-linguistic care-focus	Language reflects and shapes culture; dynamic shaping of subjectivity
	Focus on: • individual rights • autonomy • reason • fairness • reform • justice	Focus on: • bodies • reproduction • sexuality • women's culture	Focus on: • labor • wage gap • global markets • corporatization	Focus on: • multiplicity • intersectionality of identities • critiques of imperialist practices and assumptions	Focus on: • Earth-centered spiritual interactions between humans and non-human world	Focus on: • language • sexuality • "women's ways" as a strength rather than liability • connection • collaboration	Focus on: • analyzing dominant discourses and assumptions about normalcy • contradictions • difference • conflict • hybrids • ambiguity

Assumptions About Power	A resource to be redistributed	Power-over domination; Power as repressive	Power-over domination; Power as repressive	Resource, domination, Power-to Transformative	Power-to empowerment	Power-over and power-to empowerment	Power as productive
Predominant Change Goals	Redistribute power between women and men equitably.	Dismantle patriarchy's social and cultural institutions.	Dismantle both oppressive systems of capitalism and patriarchy.	Recognize and value differences among women and how women's gains for some women may come at the expense of other women; therefore, work to eradicate all forms of oppression simultaneously.	Level prestige hierarchies; focus on dislodging logics of domination that place humans as superior to all other living things.	Create female language and sexuality; disrupt dominance of phallic representations privilege the feminine as much as the masculine.	Question assumptions to avoid reinscribing another successor regime of truth. Dismantle oppressive systems of thought and develop new ways of thinking and doing that are "in process" or provisional and always open to change and improvement.

(Continued)

EXHIBIT 1 (*Continued*)

Feminist Frame	Liberal	Radical	Socialist	Multicultural/ Global/ Post-colonial	Cofeminist	Psychological • psychoanalytic • care-focused	PM/poststrux Third Wave
Example Scholars	Wollstonecraft	Firestone	Eisenstein	Hill Collins	Daly	Dinnerstein	Cixous
	Taylor	Rubin	Hartmann	Spelman	Ortner	Horney	Butler
	Mill	Millett	Young	Hooks	Shiva	Flax	Lather
	Friedan	Daly	Jaggar	Mohanty	Starhawk	Irigaray	Drake
		French	Walby	Crenshaw	Warren	Chodorow	Heywood
				Minh-ha	Mies	Kristeva	Walker
				Anzaldua		Noddings	
						Gilligan	

Sources: Allen, 1999; Kolmar and Bartkowski, 2010; Tong, 2009.

Feminist theory offers a set of lenses that have been refined over decades for the purpose of analyzing oppression and for the promotion of equity in a range of contexts, including education. For scholars and practitioners studying and working in colleges and universities and concerned about equity, feminist theory can provide sophisticated and finely tuned approaches to understanding the complexities of inequity and designing strategies to uproot its causes. As delineated in the first chapter, strategies to promote more equitable campus climates have been developed and implemented for numerous decades. Gifted scholars and practitioners alike have dedicated countless hours working toward institutional change to promote and sustain gender equity. And although substantial gains have been made, particularly in the area of access, evidence of change in other areas is often tenuous (see, for example, the research related to campus climate).

The following two chapters review the literature related to the status of women in higher education, with a focus on studies related to access, representation, and climate. Although feminist theory is implicit in much of the scholarship related to access and climate, the particular frame or school of thought is not always apparent. Further, differences between feminist frames guiding particular research questions and methodological approaches can yield dramatically different insights related to the same topic. Thus, the summaries of the following two chapters provide a brief synopsis of the literature against the backdrop of feminist theory.

Examining Women's Status: Access and Representation as Key Equity Indicators

ACCESS TO EDUCATION has long been identified as a key indicator of equity. Reflecting a liberal feminist frame, the call for access has been central to research and activism related to women's equal rights initiatives and nondiscrimination policies and legislation, including Title VII and Title IX. In higher education, access—or gaining entrée to a postsecondary institution as a student, faculty, staff member, or administrator—involves gatekeeping mechanisms of the admissions and hiring processes. Access also encompasses issues related to gaining entrée to particular arenas in postsecondary education, including, for instance, fields of study (for students), senior leadership posts, and full professorships, which frequently includes issues related to the pipeline such as educational and developmental opportunities to help women gain the credentials needed to advance professionally. These types of access issues are often described under the label "representation." Recent scholarship about access to institutions and access in particular arenas of higher education is the focus of this chapter.

In my research related to university women's commissions (Allan, 2003, 2008), I reported on a discourse of access that pervaded reports issued by these gender equity policy–related groups. This discourse was apparent by predominantly focusing on numbers of women compared with men as evidence of inequity and by arguing that women's status would be improved by adding more women to positions and activities from which they had been marginalized or excluded. It is illustrated in a 1992 report: "In fact, asked to name *one thing* the University could do to improve the status of its women workers, we say **hire more women at every level**" (Ohio State University, 1992, p. 15). Echoing similar themes, a more recent report from the American Association of University Professors (West and Curtis, 2006) reports that women's advancement to the highest ranks of the professoriate is slow (39 percent) and that if the pace continues at its current rate, it will take decades to attain parity.

This chapter reviews current scholarship that examines a range of access and representation issues as indicators of gender equity and the status of women in higher education. Although some commonalities exist across different constituencies in higher education, some important differences do as well. For this reason, I have organized the chapter by themes related to constituent groups beginning with students, then moving to faculty, staff, and administrative leaders, including trustees.

Women's Access to Postsecondary Education

Access to higher education can be conceptualized in several ways. For example, gaining access to higher education commonly implies formal admission into a particular postsecondary institution or permission to study within a particular discipline or field. However, even when women gain formal entrée to an institution or sphere within it, some research indicates that the quality of the educational experience may be inequitable or discriminatory. The following sections review women's access to higher education in terms of both entrée/admission and educational quality.

Getting into College

Before the 1980s, men constituted the majority of college students in the United States. Since then, and until recently, the growth in enrollment of women has exceeded that of men, shifting the balance since 1988 to women as the majority of undergraduate college students (Snyder, Dillow, and Hoffman, 2009; Touchton, Musil, and Campbell, 2008). Although the pace of growth in enrollments for women appears to be slowing, in 2007–08 women accounted for 57 percent of all undergraduate students, a slight decline from the 58 percent in 2003–04 (King, 2010). Current data reveal no difference in the proportions of men and women who enroll in college directly from high school, largely because of the steady progress by men between 2000 and

2007 as rates for women improved steadily in the 1990s and then leveled off (King, 2010). In 2006 roughly 66 percent of female students aged sixteen to twenty-four enrolled in college within twelve months of completing high school. These rates are on a par with men in this age group (also 66 percent) and represent net increases for both men and women over the previous decade (King, 2006).

Among college students aged twenty-five or older, women continue to maintain a majority, at 60 to 62 percent (King, 2010). For college-going rates, however, regardless of the time lapse between high school and postsecondary enrollment, rates increased for both women and men during the two decades between 1985 to 2005 (Touchton, Musil, and Campbell, 2008; Snyder, Dillon, and Hoffman, 2009). This trend was true across all racial and ethnic groups except Latinos, where the percentage of male students age twenty-four or younger continued to fall, from 45 percent at the turn of the century to 42 percent in 2007–08 (King, 2010). In sum, current data indicate the distribution of enrollment by gender has remained relatively unchanged since 2000, with the important exception of traditional-age Latino students (King, 2010). Not surprisingly, a similar gender gap exists in rates of high school completion among both native and foreign-born Latinos (King, 2010).

In general, both women and men are more likely to graduate from college today than ever before (Corbett, Hill, and St. Rose, 2008). Recent data confirm that the number of bachelor's degrees awarded is on the rise for both women and men, "indicating that women's success does not come at the expense of men" (King, 2010, p. v). Research suggests that rigor of the secondary curriculum is one of the best predictors of both enrollment and success in college (Adelman, 2006). Based on this information, since 1982 the U.S. Department of Education has collected data on the percentage of high school students completing the "New Basics" curriculum, which includes four years of English; three years each of social science, math, and science; two years of a foreign language; and at least one semester of computer science. The proportion of high school students completing this curriculum rose steadily, from 2 percent in 1982 to 31 percent in 2000, and a 2- to 4-percentage point difference occurred in the proportions of boys and girls completing this curriculum.

Access to Educational Quality

Although the proportion of women and men aged twenty-five to twenty-nine who have earned a high school credential has remained virtually equal since 1960 (King, 2006), some researchers contend girls and boys are not receiving the same quality of education in primary and secondary schools. Studies of college preparatory course completion in high school reveal girls are more likely than boys to have completed most college preparatory courses in math and science, with the exception of calculus and physics (King, 2006), although boys generally outperform girls on both verbal and math portions of the SAT (Corbett, Hill, and St. Rose, 2008). This finding has led some researchers to explore potential gender bias of standardized tests (Leonard and Jiang, 1999; Rosser, 1989), while others assert that qualitative differences in educational experiences may help to explain the gap (Sadker and Sadker, 1995; Sadker, Sadker, and Zittleman, 2009). For instance, research has documented how teachers call on boys more often, wait longer for boys' responses, and provide more precise feedback to boys in classroom settings. Moreover, when students ask for help with difficult problems presented in the classroom, teachers tend to encourage boys to persist in finding a solution for themselves but provide assistance for girls in solving the problem (Sadker, Sadker and Zittleman, 2009). These kinds of unintentional biases may be further compounded by the effects of verbal and sexual harassment beginning in elementary school (American Association of University Women, 2004) and internalized gender stereotypes. For instance, girls tend to rate themselves lower on technology ability than boys (National Coalition for Women and Girls in Education, 2002), and teachers can inadvertently fuel this misconception by attributing boys' success with technology to talent and girls' success to hard work (American Association of University Women, 2000).

Gender differences in quality of educational experiences are documented in the literature, but it is important to note that data indicate the effect of gender on educational achievement diminishes when socioeconomic status and race are factored into the equation (King, 2006, 2010; West and Curtis, 2006; Rowan-Kenyon, 2007). In a comprehensive review and analysis of enrollment trends based on data from the National Education Longitudinal Study: 1988–2000, Rowan-Kenyon (2007) found that, when controlling for other variables, students from "lower socioeconomic status are less likely than higher SES peers to gain access to college at any time" (p. 210). Similarly, in an examination of educational achievement from fourth grade to college, the American Association of University Women (Corbett, Hill, and St. Rose, 2008) concluded that although girls' and boys' educational outcomes have generally improved or remained the same, large discrepancies by race or ethnicity and family income exist. Generally speaking, children from the lowest-income families have the lowest average test scores, and even an incremental increase in family income appears to yield a correspondent rise in test scores (Corbett, Hill, and St. Rose, 2008).

Girls Need Not Apply?

As of 2007, 18.2 million students were enrolled for credit in U.S. higher education. Of that number, 57 percent were female (King, 2010). Data like these underscore strong gains for women in terms of access to higher education—which should be good news. But when gender equity is conceptualized as a zero-sum game, the overall majority status of women students in higher education can mistakenly be taken to signal that efforts to improve women's status in higher education are no longer needed. Indeed, Glazer-Raymo explains how the catalyst for her *Unfinished Agendas: New and Continuing Gender Challenges in Higher Education* (2008b) was in part a new form of gender bias fueled by efforts to view the majority status of women students in many settings as a problem. This new form of bias results in a scenario where "rather than being applauded for their academic achievements, women have become victims of their success, as beneficiaries of laws and regulations that are now being called into question" (p. 2). Such perspectives are occasionally expressed in the popular press but have also shaped recent scholarship. For instance, in a recent article published in *Higher Education Management and Policy*, the authors urge colleges to shift practices toward more rigorous recruiting of male students because in their view, the increased proportion of female students is a "serious problem" for higher education institutions (Evers, Livernois, and Mancuso, 2006, p. 12).

Moreover, some sources indicate that among colleges and universities with more selective admissions processes, the rise in female applications and admissions over the past decade has resulted in women experiencing a lower rate of admission than their male counterparts as these institutions attempt to maintain a gender balance in the student body. Accordingly, "female applicants have faced an admission rate that is an average of 13 percentage points lower than that of their male peers just for the sake of keeping that girl-boy balance" (Kingsbury, 2007, p. 50). Further, officials at some of these institutions report that maintaining a balance between male and female students often requires a "thumb on the scale in favor of boys" as girls, from the earliest grades, tend to be better students, earn better grades, and participate in more extracurricular activities than their male counterparts (Kingsbury, 2007). Thus, it appears that less accomplished males may have an advantage over more accomplished females in seeking admission to selective colleges (Jaschik, 2006). Although these types of reports can contribute to shaping a perception that boys are now disadvantaged in higher education, data reveal that college enrollments have remained steady or have increased among men.

Representation of Women Students in Higher Education

Representation of women in higher education is multifaceted. Enrollment and degree attainment data provide a starting point for examining the representation of women students.

Enrollment

College-going rates of women are generally considered a mark of success on the path toward gender equity. As noted, recent data confirm that women continue to pursue postsecondary education in record numbers—also true across racial and ethnic groups for which data are available (King, 2010). In some cases, these gains for women have been framed as a loss or "crisis" for male students despite the fact that there has been no less attainment in college enrollments by white men and college enrollments for men of color have also increased. Thus, the number of men enrolling in college has remained steady (for whites) or increased (for men of color except Latinos); however, the rate of college attendance by women has grown to exceed that of men, and it is this trend that has resulted in an overall increase in the proportion of female students relative to male (King, 2006, 2010). In sum, when considered in the aggregate, more men and women are enrolling in college than ever before, and the proportion of young men graduating from high school and earning college degrees is, according to the American Association of University Women, at an all-time high. The rate of increase for women, however, exceeds that for men, resulting in a higher proportion of female students (Snyder, Dillow, and Hoffman, 2009). Increases in postsecondary enrollment for both women and men are expected to continue; current projections by the U.S. Department of Education indicate enrollment will increase by about 16 percent for women and 9 percent for men by 2018 (Hussar and Bailey, 2009).

Enrollment and student age data reveal that among undergraduate students older than twenty-four, women account for nearly twice as many students (22.1 percent) as men (14 percent; King, 2010). Researchers point to lifelong implications of a cohort of women who are entering their earning years without a bachelor's degree, resulting in potential gender-based disparities in future income, retirement savings, and accumulated capital—for the remainder of their lives. Unfortunately, studies confirm that even when women earn a bachelor's degree earlier, their earnings over time (on average) continue to be less than their male counterparts, which disparity can be further magnified for those carrying significant student loans (Webster and Bishaw, 2007).

Although studies affirm that gender, race, and ethnicity are important variables influencing educational outcomes, volumes of data underscore that higher family income may be the most salient factor correlated with increased likelihood of educational achievement (Sax and Harper, 2007; Touchton, Musil, and Campbell, 2008). The link between family income and educational achievement has been documented in numerous studies of educational outcomes from childhood through postsecondary education (Mortenson, 2007). When data are disaggregated by sex, however, women account for the majority of lower-income college students. Further, across racial and ethnic groups, the gender gap in undergraduate enrollment narrows as family income rises. For example, male students were 44 percent of dependent graduates in the lowest income quartile but accounted for 52 percent of undergraduates in the highest quartile (King, 2006). These data may in part explain why men are less likely than women to reenter higher education later in life, as men of all educational levels continue to command higher salaries in the labor market (King, 2010; Webster and Bishaw, 2007).

Degree Attainment

Women have become the majority of degree earners in nearly every level of postsecondary education except Ph.D. and M.D. programs; men earn the majority of these degrees (King, 2010). Although the total number of degrees awarded to both men and women has increased over the last decade, the number of degrees awarded to women (among whites and minorities) has increased at a higher rate (King, 2006; Touchton, Musil, and Campbell, 2008), with undergraduate degree attainment among women leveling off between 2006 and 2010 (King, 2010). Women are heavily concentrated in particular fields, however, earning a majority of their degrees in health professions, psychology, education, other social sciences, and the humanities. Across degree fields, women as a group earn 62 percent of associate degrees, 58 percent of bachelor's degrees, 60 percent of master's degrees, 50 percent of first professional degrees, and 45 percent of doctorates (see Figure 1; King, 2010).

Differences in degree attainment by race must be considered when examining women's status in higher education. In 2005 white women accounted for 34 percent of the total U.S. population; minority women 17 percent. In that same time period, white women earned 39 percent of associate and bachelor's degrees; minority women 18 and 14 percent, respectively. In addition, white women earned 37 percent and minority women 12 percent of master's degrees, and white women earned 33 percent and minority women 13 percent of professional degrees. Although minority men are earning more degrees at every level than ten years ago, minority women are earning a higher proportion of degrees at a faster rate than their male counterparts (Cook and Cordova, 2007).

When considered in the aggregate, women currently attain the majority of college degrees across types of postsecondary institutions. More specifically, they earn 57 percent of degrees at public baccalaureate institutions, 61 percent at public associate degree–granting institutions, and 62 percent at private not-for-profit two-year institutions (Snyder, Dillow, and Hoffman, 2008).

FIGURE 1
Representation of Women Degree Earners

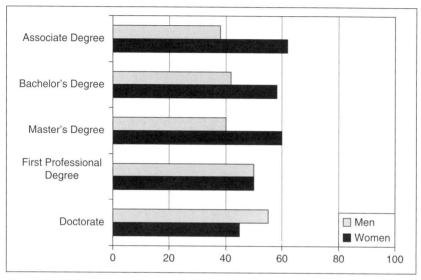

Source: King, 2010.

In many disciplines, women are either the majority of degree earners or roughly on par with men (see Figure 2).

When disaggregated by discipline, data reveal that in most of the science, technology, engineering, and mathematics (STEM) fields, women earn less than half of the degrees awarded. Some notable exceptions include gains in agricultural sciences (51 percent), biological sciences (62 percent), and psychology (78 percent); up 11, 9, and 5 percentage points, respectively, since 1996 (National Science Foundation, 2007). In other fields, however, the realities are not so encouraging. Women earned only 20 percent of bachelor's degrees in engineering and 22 percent in computer science in 2009. Further, the most recent data indicate a trend of reduced participation of women that holds across almost every discipline in the STEM fields, from undergraduate to graduate levels and beyond (National Science Foundation, 2007). Reward structures, students' value systems, pedagogical approaches, and lack of role

FIGURE 2
Women Students by Institutional Type

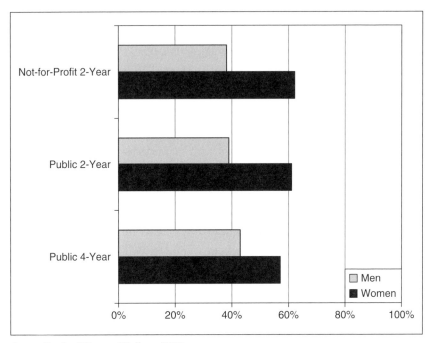

Source: Snyder, Dillow, and Hoffman, 2008.

models may pose potential barriers for women in these fields (Goulden, Frasch, and Mason, 2009; S. V. Rosser, 2004, 2007). Research about why particular fields are less successful than others in advancing women's status is explored further in the next chapter.

In sum, although persistent and complex problems continue to hinder equitable representation of women in STEM fields, overall, more women than ever before are earning degrees in U.S. colleges and universities at nearly all levels and in all types of institutions. When aggregate numbers are the sole measure, the increasing proportion of women in higher education is occasionally framed as a threat to men (Evers, Livernois, and Mancuso, 2006), yet data confirm that more men (with the exception of Latino men) are enrolling in and obtaining college degrees than ever before (King, 2010). Drawing conclusions about the attainment of equity for women students based on overall numbers of women who have gained access to higher education belies important nuances related to their representation across fields of study, in particular in the STEM fields, where career opportunities tend to provide higher salaries than many other fields.

Cocurricular Representation

In addition to examining the representation of women students by field of study, examining their representation in other arenas of student life is also part of establishing a more complete picture of the status of women students in higher education.

Student Leadership

In general, research suggests that student involvement in cocurricular activities has a positive effect on educational persistence and attainment and strong positive effects on self-concept (Astin, 1984; Pascarella and Terenzini, 2005). Research with a specific focus on gender in cocurricular activities (other than athletics) is thin. *Women in Higher Education: An Encyclopedia* (Langdon, 2002) provides an overview of scholarship related to women and the cocurriculum, noting that gender is rarely addressed in the landmark, large-scale studies of how the cocurriculum contributes to learning. Pascarella and Terenzini (2005) report that women who took a leadership role in cocurricular activities were more likely to select careers in male-dominated fields. In general, however, studies indicate that women are underrepresented in higher-status leadership roles on coeducational campuses (Astin, 1993; Valian, 1999). Astin's research (1977, 1993) has revealed that attending a women's college has a positive effect on many leadership outcomes for women. Smaller studies, like a recent dissertation (Vander Hooven, 2009), found that even among women attending a community college while also parenting children, cocurricular involvement was perceived to positively affect the attainment of an associate's degree.

Recent research reveals differences by gender and type of cocurricular participation. For instance, in a study of undergraduate student government leaders at twenty-one comprehensive universities in the Midwest, Miller and

Kraus (2004) found that although women held nearly half (47.9 percent) of student government positions, the majority of students holding the highest-ranking leadership positions were male. More specifically, 71.4 percent of student government presidents and vice presidents were male, and of the 105 chances for a woman to be elected as student government president over the last five years, women were elected twenty-seven times (25.7 percent; p. 425).

Gendered patterns of behavior were also revealed in analyses of data from the National Survey of Student Engagement; Kinzie and colleagues (n.d.) report that "gender gaps expose qualitatively different undergraduate experiences for men and women," regardless of institutional type (p. 21). The report concludes that women students are more likely than their male counterparts to participate in activities that complement and enrich academic curricula (like study abroad and attending arts events), while male undergraduates are more likely than women to be involved with cocurricular activities and exercise. These findings complement other studies that have documented the greater likelihood of women's participation in study abroad (Institute of International Education, 2010) and service-learning activities (Campus Compact, 2003) than their male peers.

Athletics

Alongside student organizations, clubs, and student government, athletics represents another arena of cocurricular involvement where data have been analyzed. Women's increased participation in intercollegiate athletics has been a much-publicized outcome of Title IX enforcement since its passage in 1972. Indeed, in 2010 women's participation in college sports was near the highest level ever, involving more than 180,000 female athletes in 9,087 women's collegiate teams—an increase of 1,586 teams over the last decade (Acosta and Carpenter, 2010, p. 16). The attainment of gender equity in athletics under Title IX applies not only to opportunities to participate in sports but also to equal opportunity in terms of scholarships, benefits, facilities, and other resources related to athletic participation. Recent decisions by the Department of Education, however, have weakened the enforcement of Title IX by shifting the burden of proof for compliance with Title IX to the female athletes rather than to the institutions in which they are enrolled (Glazer-Raymo, 2008a). In 2002, the thirtieth anniversary of the passage of Title IX, women accounted for 42 percent of college varsity athletes—a substantial increase over the mere 15 percent in 1972. The number of opportunities for women to participate in sports has necessarily expanded over time. For instance, in 1970 there were 2.5 women's teams per institution, compared with 8.6 in 2010 (Acosta and Carpenter, 2010, p. 10). The "vast majority of institutions remain out of compliance" with Title IX, however (Anderson, Cheslock, and Ehrenberg, 2006, p. 225). Moreover, recent research reveals that improved gender equity (in terms of closing the proportionality gap) for women student athletes is much slower than previously thought, especially when data are adjusted to ensure consistent reporting methods (Anderson, Cheslock, and Ehrenberg, 2006).

Importantly, in both high school (where growth has been parallel) and college, the increase in female participants has occurred without interfering with the growth of male participants (Acosta and Carpenter, 2010, p. 11). "The depth of resistance to women's full participation in intercollegiate sport," however, historically and even today has been observed by many and explored in scholarly examinations (see, for example, Estler and Nelson, 2005; Festle, 1996; Hoffman, Iverson, Allan, and Ropers-Huilman, 2010; Suggs, 2008). Currently, if all female varsity athletes in high school wanted to play in college, only one in seventeen could be accommodated because of the limited number of teams available for women (Acosta and Carpenter, 2010).

Although proportions of female athletes and increased participation opportunities represent some advancement toward equity, they do not accurately represent its attainment. If women were represented proportionally to their enrollment, they would have been 55 percent of varsity athletes in 2002 and 57 percent in 2008 (Anderson, Cheslock, and Ehrenberg, 2006; Glazer-Raymo, 2008a; King, 2010). In an investigation of Title IX compliance reported in 2006, researchers found 71 to 83 percent of institutions did *not* meet the criteria of substantial proportionality; that is, the proportion of female undergraduates at the institution was more than 3 to 5 percent larger than the proportion of female varsity athletes. The researchers found that the most improvement in compliance between 1995 and 2002 was among Division I institutions. More specifically, in Division I the more selective institutions, larger institutions, and those with higher tuition and fees had smaller proportionality gaps. Wider gaps were associated with institutions having a larger share of female undergraduates and those institutions with a football team (Anderson, Cheslock, and Ehrenberg, 2006).

According to a 2009 report from the Institute for Diversity and Ethics in Sport, gender and racial diversity in college sports is declining, described by Richard Lapchick, its primary author and director of the institute, as "the worst report card for college sport in many years" (Sander, 2009). The report documented "a lack of overall progress in college sport," including "a decline in both racial and gender hiring practices in key positions" (Sander, 2009). The representation of women as coaches and athletic administrators is discussed in more detail later in this chapter.

Graduate Students

Graduate degrees are seen as gateways to academic careers. In 2005–06, women earned more than half of all doctorates in education (65 percent), social sciences (57 percent), life sciences (52 percent), and humanities (51 percent) while remaining greatly underrepresented in the physical sciences (28 percent), engineering (20 percent), and business (39 percent; Hoffer, Hess, Welch, and Williams, 2007). Although the percentages are much lower in physical sciences and engineering, it is noteworthy that these figures represent substantial increases over the previous thirty to forty years. Overall, women earn about 45 percent of all doctoral degrees awarded in the United States, and of these graduates, 27 percent are white, 10 percent Asian American, 3 percent African American, 2 percent Latina, 2 percent American Indian, and 4 percent unknown (see Figure 3; Hoffer and others, 2007).

More women than men reported plans to use their doctoral education in a teaching career, while men with doctorates were more likely to report attaining careers in research and development in business and industry. Women were also more likely to enter administration or provide professional services to individuals (Hoffer and others, 2007). Interestingly, about 14 percent of all doctoral degree recipients began their postsecondary education in community colleges, with women somewhat more likely (16 percent) to do so than their male counterparts (13 percent).

FIGURE 3
Women Doctoral Recipients by Race

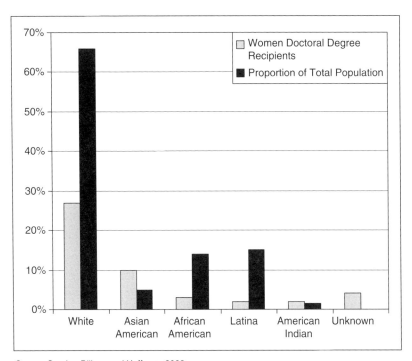

Source: Snyder, Dillow, and Hoffman, 2009.

In other gender differences related to doctoral degree recipients, Mason and Goulden's research (2004) indicates gender differences among Ph.D.s working in academia who have "early babies" (those born up to five years after completing a doctorate). More specifically, the data indicate men who have early babies are 38 percent more likely than their female counterparts to achieve tenure (Mason and Goulden, 2004). Touchton, Musil, and Campbell (2008) suggest this fact may account for some of the later gender disparity in academic careers, with only 56 percent of women still working in academia twelve years after achieving tenure compared with 77 percent of men (p. 18). Women who leave the tenure track often end up working as lecturers, adjuncts, and part timers with lower salaries and less job security.

Faculty

U.S. colleges and universities currently employ approximately 3.6 million individuals. Of that number, approximately 1.4 million are faculty members, 2.6 are professional staff, and nearly 1 million serve in nonprofessional staff roles (Snyder and Dillow, 2010). Gender equity and the status of women have been explored to varying degrees in each of these populations. Overall, numbers and proportions of women serving as faculty members in postsecondary institutions have risen substantially over previous decades. When considering the growth in light of the available pool, however, scholars have characterized the pace of progress toward equitable gender representation among faculty as "excruciatingly slow" (Valian, 1999), "glacial" (Glazer-Raymo, 1999), and exemplifying "demographic inertia" (Hargens and Long, 2002; Marschke, Laursen, Nielsen, and Rankin, 2007). In 2007 women accounted for 46 percent of full-time faculty members in the United States (Snyder and Dillow, 2010). Yet women rarely represent more than 30 percent of full-time tenure-track faculty at research extensive universities. Although such universities constitute a relatively small portion (6.4 percent) of all postsecondary institutions in the United States, they are generally considered to set a standard in academia (Bok, 1990) and enjoy substantial influence as chief beneficiaries of financial support from public and private sources.

Assuming that overall growth in the number of women faculty constitutes a clear-cut indicator of progress toward gender equity can eclipse the fact that women account for a disproportionate share of contingent faculty or non-tenure-track (lecturers, instructors) and part-time appointments (American Federation of Teachers, 2009, p. 20; Glazer-Raymo, 2008a; Snyder and Dillow, 2010). In terms of gender equity, this trend is significant in that these positions tend to be the least secure, least well paid, and least prestigious among faculty ranks in higher education (West and Curtis, 2006). In sum, women account for more than half of all lecturers (52 percent) and instructors (54 percent) and 47 percent of assistant professors, yet they constitute only 39 percent of associate and 25 percent of full professors (Snyder, Dillow, and Hoffman, 2008). Two-year colleges have the most female faculty and research universities the least. More specifically, the distribution of women

FIGURE 4
Percentage of Women Faculty by Institutional Type

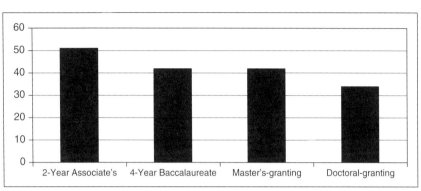

Source: Snyder, Dillow, and Hoffman, 2009.

among the faculty by type of institution and rank resembles an inverted funnel inversely proportional to established prestige hierarchies in U.S. higher education (see Figure 4).

The following general conclusions have been drawn about women's representation among faculty in higher education:

The highest degree of parity is in two-year colleges, the lowest in research universities and selective liberal arts colleges.

Part-time faculty appointments are on the rise, but women account for a far greater share of them.

Of full-time faculty appointments, women account for 39 percent, while men account for 61 percent.

Higher proportions of women are being hired in non-tenure-track jobs, where advancement is limited in terms of salary and rank.

In 2005–2006 women were 24 percent of all full professors (compared with 10 percent in 1974–1975).

As well, salaries continue to lag behind those for male counterparts across all ranks and types of institutions (see the following chapter; Touchton, Musil, and Campbell, 2008; Snyder, Dillow, and Hoffman, 2009).

FIGURE 5
Percentage of Full-Time Female Faculty by Discipline

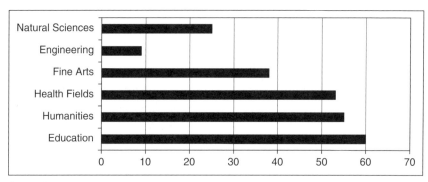

Source: Snyder, Tan, and Hoffman, 2006.

Along with institutional differences, full-time women faculty are more likely to be found in particular disciplines. Women are most likely to be faculty in education (60 percent of full-time faculty are women), humanities (55 percent), health fields (53 percent), and fine arts (38 percent; see Figure 5). They are least likely to be professors of engineering (9 percent), and the natural sciences (25 percent; Knapp, Kelly-Reld, Whitmore, and Miller, 2007).

Further, it has been established that female-dominated fields such as education, English, psychology, nursing, and social work pay less than male-dominated fields (Bellas, 1993). Although both men and women who work in these fields earn lower salaries, research indicates that the women's salaries are slightly lower than comparable men in the same field (Bellas, 1993). These fields also tend to attract less external funding to support faculty research and perks like travel to conferences and purchase of computers and other technology (Cooper and others, 2007). These and other issues related to salary equity are discussed further in the following chapter.

The slow rate of posttenure advancement has prompted numerous questions guiding investigations designed to examine factors contributing to the apparent "stall-out" problem in academia (Shaw, 2007): a focus on sufficient and transparent policies to support women's advancement to full professor, individual discrimination and climate-related issues, mentoring, access to leadership opportunities, and funding to gain the requisite qualifications needed to be promoted. These issues, along with salary equity for faculty, are described in more detail in the next chapter.

Women Staff in Higher Education

Those working in noninstructional and nonadministrative roles—whether professional, clerical, technical, or some other capacity—are often overlooked in examinations of workforce issues in higher education. Scholarship related to gender equity is no exception. For this reason, these higher education support personnel have been referred to as the "hidden workforce," as administrators or scholars pay relatively little attention to understanding or improving their work lives (Rhoades and Maitland, 1998; Johnsrud, 2002; Rhoades, 2000).

Numbers of noninstructional staff employed in U.S. higher education grew 20 percent from 1997 to 2007 (American Federation of Teachers, 2009). As the proportion of part-time contingent faculty increased during that decade, the opposite trend occurred for noninstructional staff, declining among part-time staff (18 to 15 percent) and increasing for full-time staff (82 to 85 percent). The greatest gains were among professional and administrative positions, which grew 54 percent and 41 percent, respectively (American Federation of Teachers, 2009), whereas other categories (technical, clerical, skilled crafts) remained relatively stable or experienced slight declines.

Among education support personnel, women continued to account for the vast majority of clerical and secretarial positions (86.6 percent) and were vastly outnumbered by men in the skilled crafts group (6.9 percent compared with 93.1 percent). Sixty percent of technical or paraprofessional staff were women, whereas the reverse was true for the service or maintenance category, where men accounted for 61.8 percent and women for 38.2 percent. In every occupational group, including the clerical or secretarial category, men earned more than women, and in three of five occupational categories of education support personnel, men were awarded higher percentage increases than their female counterparts (see Figure 6; Johnsrud, 2002).

Among women who work in faculty and salaried or professional positions, the invisible barriers to advancement rooted in sexism are known as the "glass

FIGURE 6
Percentage of Women Higher Education Support Personnel

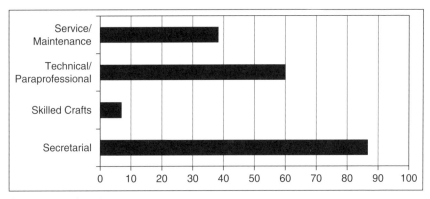

Source: Johnsrud, 2002.

ceiling." It is rare for women working in low-wage jobs to even encounter the glass ceiling, however, as these positions tend to offer few changes for mobility or advancement. The constraints to occupational advancement encountered by women in clerical and secretarial roles have come to be known as the "sticky floor" (Noble, 1992; Miller, 2008). Despite the obstacles, however, some clerical and secretarial staff do make the transition to professional staff roles. Such a progression can involve numerous challenges, however, as detailed by Iverson (2009) in her study of twenty-two women who had moved from secretarial to professional roles in a university setting. In the process of making this transition, participants encountered structural and institutional barriers rooted in attitudes about gender and what it means to be "professional" that impeded their mobility and access to higher-wage jobs or professional positions.

Athletics Staff

Although the participation of undergraduate women in intercollegiate athletics remains near its highest levels ever, the representation of women coaches is low. In 2010, 42.6 percent of women's teams had a female head coach, and less than 3 percent of men's teams were coached by women; combined, only 20.9 percent of all teams had a woman as head coach (Carpenter and Acosta,

56

2010). These figures represent considerable regression since 1972, when more than 90 percent of women's teams and about 2 percent of men's teams had a female head coach (Carpenter and Acosta, 2010). Currently, men coach nearly 80 percent of all intercollegiate teams, and 57.4 percent of head coaches for women's teams are male (Carpenter and Acosta, 2010). Scholars have explored this downward trend in gender equity: "The irony of Title IX is that its enactment was one response to feminist activism and that it resulted in the subordination of women's sports to the dominant male model" (Estler and Nelson, 2005, p. 61). Gendered assumptions about who is most likely to have expertise in the realm of athletics, masculine models of leadership, and homophobia have been offered by scholars as explanations for the regression in women's leadership of women's intercollegiate sports (Estler and Nelson, 2005; Griffin, 1998; Messner and Sabo, 1990).

Despite this regression, gains have occurred at the assistant coach level, where 57.6 percent of women's teams have paid assistant coaches who are women. This percentage represents an increase of 2,698 paid female assistant coaches since 1996. Importantly, the percentages need to be understood in light of the total numbers. Because more colleges and universities have developed athletics programs, the number of jobs in athletics administration has more than doubled since 1988. Between 2008 and 2010, the overall number of positions increased by five, with women holding 536 fewer of these jobs and men 541 more than they did in 2008 (Carpenter and Acosta, 2010, p. 37).

Data relative to the representation of women as athletic trainers and sports information directors provide further insight about the status of women in terms of access and representation in professional roles in higher education. As of 2010, more than 90 percent of all NCAA member institutions provided athletic training services for their athletes, yet only 28 percent of head athletic trainers were women. And, although nearly all colleges and universities with athletic programs had a sports information director, only 11.9 percent of them were female (Carpenter and Acosta, 2010, pp. 38–40).

Senior Administrators

Overall, gains for women in the senior ranks of college and university administration have been substantial; in the aggregate across types of postsecondary institutions, women account for 45 percent of all senior administrators. This percentage represents considerable growth over the two decades between 1986, when they were only 10 percent of all college presidents and 2006, when they accounted for 23 percent. Although these gains are encouraging, a closer examination of the data reveals that gendered prestige hierarchies noted for faculty are also present at senior administrative levels. In fact, community colleges are the only type of postsecondary institution where women hold more than half (52 percent) of senior leadership positions (King and Gomez, 2008; Touchton, Musil, and Campbell, 2008).

As senior administrators, women are most likely to be found at two-year institutions, and across types of institutions, they are more likely to serve in student affairs, external affairs, or administrative affairs than academic affairs—and they are most numerous in positions as chief of staff and chief diversity officer (Touchton, Musil, and Campbell, 2008). Women remain underrepresented in academic leadership positions (department chairs and academic deans), in both absolute numbers and in proportion to the eligible pool of tenured women (Dominici, Fried, and Zeger, 2009). The areas where women tend to be more highly represented also tend to be the lowest-paying administrative posts. Further, chief academic officer positions, the most common springboard to the presidency, remain heavily dominated by white men, especially at research universities (King and Gomez, 2008).

Athletics Directors

The representation of women in senior leadership positions (athletic directors, associate directors, and assistant directors) in intercollegiate athletics administration, alongside their representation as head coaches, has regressed over the years. In 1972 when Title IX was enacted, women were senior administrators of more than 90 percent of women's intercollegiate athletics programs—though they rarely led programs that included men's teams. Today the landscape has changed dramatically, and women do administer athletics programs that include men's teams. And although the gains have been slight, as of 2010 more women held administrative posts in athletics than at any time since the 1970s. Although women represent more than 57 percent of undergraduate students and approximately 35 percent of athletics administrative staffs, however, they are only 19.3

percent of athletics directors (Carpenter and Acosta, 2010, p. 36). Again, the phrase "the higher the fewer" describes the situation for women in athletics administration.

Although the average number of athletics administrators per program was at its highest level in 2010 (3.78), more than 13 percent of athletics programs had administrative structures that did not include any women among the leadership ranks (Carpenter and Acosta, 2010, p. 37). Among the 331 Division I athletics programs, only twenty-nine senior athletic directors were women (8.8 percent), and of them, only 1.3 percent were women of color (Lapchick, 2009). Scholars have offered a number of explanations for the barriers to women's advancing to the most senior positions in intercollegiate athletics, including homologous reproduction (when the dominant group seeks to replicate itself based on social and physical characteristics; Sagas and Cunningham, 2004; Sagas, Cunningham, and Teed, 2006; Stangl and Kane, 1991) and the strength of the old boy network (Grappendorf, Pent, Burton, and Henderson, 2008; Lovett and Lowry, 1994), where women are at a disadvantage in garnering the qualifications of managing resources (related to football specifically) and are then perceived as lacking credibility as legitimate candidates (Hoffman, forthcoming).

College and University Presidents

More than six hundred women serve as chief executives of colleges and universities in the United States—roughly 23 percent of the total as of 2008. This figure represents substantial growth since 1975, when only 148 college presidents were women. Further, as a group, women college and university presidents are more diverse, with 19 percent of female presidents women of color compared with 12 percent of male presidents who were men of color (Cook and Cordova, 2007). Over the last decade, however, appointments of women to college presidencies have slowed. Currently, more women and women of color are in the pipeline than are being selected for these chief executive positions (Cook and Cordova, 2007; Touchton, Musil, and Campbell, 2008).

Despite challenges and barriers women have faced, they have made substantial headway in many respects. For instance, when data were gathered in 1975, almost 90 percent of women presidents were in small private colleges, many of them women's colleges (Bornstein, 2008). In comparison, women today lead many different types of institutions—large, small, urban, rural, public, private (Touchton, Musil, and Campbell, 2008). Although the progress is commendable, women are still more likely to serve as presidents of community colleges, women's colleges, or comprehensive colleges than in more prestigious research universities (Eddy, 2002; American Council on Education, 2010). More specifically, female presidents are more likely to be in public than private institutions and more likely to head associate degree–granting (29 percent) than baccalaureate (23 percent) institutions and are least represented at doctoral-granting (14 percent) institutions (Cook and Cordova, 2007).

In addition to issues of the pipeline, scholars have cited similar barriers to those facing women candidates for senior athletic directors; that is, qualified women may be passed over for such posts because of their nontraditional backgrounds (for example, slower career trajectories because they have taken time off for family) and perceptions that they are not as well prepared for the position compared with male candidates in the pool (Bornstein, 2008). These findings may in part explain why considerably more male presidents are likely to be married (89 percent to 63 percent) and have children (91 percent to 68 percent) than women college and university presidents (Bornstein, 2008; Touchton, Musil, and Campbell, 2008). Further, even single women are likely to shoulder more responsibility as care providers and household managers than their male counterparts, and "given the long ascension to the presidency, these role conflicts can slow down progress for women" (Eddy, 2002, p. 501).

When a woman is able to overcome obstacles thwarting her career path and gender biases in search processes, she often continues to face legitimacy hurdles, especially when presiding over institutions with Division I athletic programs and medical schools where "these high-cost, high-maintenance programs have vocal boosters and detractors who require a great deal of a president's attention and tend to be uncomfortable dealing with women executives" (Bornstein, 2008, p. 170). According to Molly Broad, president of the American Council on Education and past president of the University of North Carolina system, the "dearth of female college presidents comes down to the hiring process," where the old boy network provides an advantage to male candidates who are hired by boards of trustees who are primarily white men (Brown, 2009).

Nevertheless, women continue to succeed; over the last decade, a number of prominent women scholars have achieved appointments as presidents of major research universities: Drew Gilpin Faust, Harvard University (2007); Mary Sue Coleman, University of Michigan (2002); Amy Gutmann, University of Pennsylvania (2005); Susan Hockfield, MIT (2004); Ruth Simmons, Brown University (2001); Lou Anna Simon, Michigan State University (2005); and Shirley Tilghman, Princeton University (2004; Glazer-Raymo, 2008b, 2008c).

Women and Governing Boards

Governing boards or boards of trustees of higher education institutions are the top of the organizational hierarchies of colleges and universities, working directly with the president or chancellor of an institution or university system. Some fifty thousand individuals currently serve as trustees of higher education governing boards in the United States. They are often corporate or civic leaders, benefactors, alumnae, or alumni (Glazer-Raymo, 2008c). "Eighty-six percent of women and 91 percent of men reported being major donors to the institutions on whose boards they serve" (Scollay, Bratt, and Tickamyer, 1996, cited in Glazer-Raymo, 2008c, p. 195).

Glazer-Raymo's analysis, "Women on Governing Boards: Why Gender Matters" (2008c), provides a thorough and helpful overview of the historical and current context of women trustees. Additionally, the Association of Governing Boards (AGB) publishes information and resources about college and university governance, the role of trustees, and demographics of trustees. According to the AGB, women account for 29 percent of trustees on the boards of public institutions and a slightly higher percentage (30 percent) on boards of independent institutions (Association of Governing Boards, 2010a, 2010b). Importantly, however, Glazer-Raymo (2008c) notes that data for private-sector membership is skewed by the high proportion of women (63 percent) who serve on boards of women's colleges. When this group is excluded, women account for only 27 percent of the membership of private boards.

Boards are also predominantly white (78 percent of public boards and 88 percent of boards for independent institutions), the majority of trustees are fifty to sixty-nine years of age, and 51 percent have careers in business-related fields (Association of Governing Boards, 2010a, 2010b; Schwartz and Atkins, 2004). In terms of leadership on governing boards, women are most likely to chair governing boards of community colleges (30.3 percent) and least likely to chair boards of multicampus systems (13.2 percent; Glazer-Raymo, 2008c, p. 195). Similar to explanations noted in previous sections on women in administrative and leadership roles, scholars have advanced three primary arguments to explain the gender imbalances in governing boards: lack of qualified women in the pipeline; inefficiency of markets; and conflicts between family and work (Glazer-Raymo, 2008a; 2008c). In her interviews with women trustees, Glazer-Raymo (2008c) found that "the perpetuation of masculine stereotypes that continue to set the standard of effective leadership" continues to serve as a major barrier for women in the trustee environment (p. 202).

Summary

Women have made impressive gains in their access to and representation in higher education. The greatest movement toward parity in terms of numbers is among students, where women currently account for 57 percent of undergraduate students and are pursuing degrees in a range of disciplines across virtually every type of postsecondary institution. In fact, women have become the majority of degree earners in nearly every level of postsecondary education except Ph.D. and M.D. programs (King, 2010). But women are heavily concentrated in particular fields, earning a majority of their degrees in health professions, psychology, education, other social sciences, and the humanities. Further, on the whole, white women have been the primary beneficiaries of affirmative action (Cooper and Stevens, 2002). Although white women are 34 percent and minority women are 17 percent of the general population, white women earned 39 percent of associate and bachelor's degrees; minority women 18 and 14 percent, respectively. At the graduate level, white women earned 37 percent of master's degrees and 33 percent of professional degrees, while minority women earned 12 percent and 13 percent of those degrees (Cook and Cordova, 2007).

The persistence of gender-related patterns of inequity is noted in research related to student access and engagement in cocurricular activities. Some research indicates women are less likely than their male counterparts to be involved in activities and be elected to the most senior positions in student government (Kinzie and others, n.d.; Miller and Kraus, 2004). Research is needed in this area, however, to document and explore these differences in more depth. Substantial strides have been made in expanding opportunities for women students in intercollegiate athletics, where women account for roughly 42 percent of all intercollegiate athletes. Yet more work is needed to attain representation that is on a par with their proportion of the undergraduate population (57 percent; Acosta and Carpenter, 2010).

The representation of faculty, staff, and administrators in higher education is aptly described as "the higher, the fewer." Persistent gaps remain in equity for women in higher-ranking positions such as full professorships or provost positions and in the more prestigious types of institutions like doctoral-granting research universities. For instance, women are most likely to be tenured faculty in associate degree–granting institutions (51 percent) and least likely in doctoral-granting institutions (34 percent; Snyder and Dillow, 2010; Touchton, Musil, and Campbell, 2008). The same trends are found for the representation of women as senior administrators, presidents, and members of governing boards (Cook and Cordova, 2007; Glazer-Raymo, 2008c; King and Gomez, 2008; Touchton, Musil, and Campbell, 2008).

Research available indicates that although progress has been made toward achieving the equitable representation of women in U.S. higher education, persistent gaps remain and are amplified for women of color. More research is needed to analyze gaps across identity differences like race, sexual identity, disability, and age and to better understand factors that both impede and accelerate the pace of change along the path to truly equitable representation for women students, staff, faculty, and administrators in higher education. Findings reviewed in this chapter emerged from investigations designed in response to specific questions—and, like any research questions, they reflect particular conceptual frameworks and underlying assumptions. The scholarship related to access and representation is primarily conceptualized in a liberal feminist frame with a focus on individual rights, justice, and fairness and ultimately on advancing women's place in higher education by gaining increased access and status in predominantly male domains and sharing positional power equal to their male counterparts. In addition to a liberal feminist lens, the influence of multicultural or race-conscious feminism is also evident in some of this literature. Examples were seen in studies describing how identity differences among women, including race and socioeconomic status, contribute to shaping patterns of inequitable representation such that white women and students with higher family income have benefited most from gains in access and representation. Radical feminist influences are occasionally evident when scholars discuss or theorize about why women are under- or overrepresented in various fields or arenas. For instance, researchers may point to the presence of an old boy network or the persistence of masculine norms and hierarchies as impediments to women pursuing particular fields or attaining certain types of leadership roles. These types of assessments hint at the radical feminist view of patriarchy and male oppression as the most salient explanation of gender inequity. Nevertheless, the literature reviewed in this chapter was not focused on dismantling patriarchal systems inherent in the infrastructure of male-dominated organizations. Rather, the research questions guiding this literature are reform-oriented primarily and focus on describing women's presence in higher education and then advocating for a more even distribution of power and resources in institutions of higher education.

Examining Women's Status: Campus Climate and Gender Equity

CAMPUS CLIMATE PROVIDES ANOTHER GAUGE for assessing progress toward the attainment of equity. Climate encompasses a range of factors, some of which are quantifiable, like salary disparities, and others of which are more qualitative in nature and involve aspects of institutional climate and culture that contribute to women's individual and collective experiences of feeling devalued, marginalized, and at times unsafe as a result of persistent problems with sexual harassment and assault. Over the past two decades especially, these sometimes subtle but no less powerful equity indicators have been documented in a myriad of ways. For instance, the following excerpt from a 1992 report illustrates an effort to frame equity in terms of institutional culture and climate: "The very fabric of the institution, how we do business, must change in order for women to advance, to be successful, and thus to make their maximum contribution to the university. . . . Our most difficult challenge may well be not to change numbers, not even to change structures, but to change the deeply and often unconsciously sexist attitudes that pervade women's experience of those numbers and structures (Ohio State University, 1992, p. 10).

More recently, an article in *The Chronicle of Higher Education* reported, "Women who do get hired at major research universities often find a 'toxic atmosphere'" (Wilson, 2004, p. 1). Research has found that women faculty report experiencing more stress than their male counterparts related to core aspects of faculty work, including teaching loads, publishing and research demands, and review and promotion processes where performance assessments can be gendered.

As introduced in the first chapter, the concept of *climate* refers to the temporal and somewhat dynamic perceived qualities of the immediate classroom or institutional environment that emerge from the complex transaction of many variables (dynamics, forces). Campus climates are intended to be positive for all members of the campus community, but in practice, they range from hostile, toxic, and chilly to welcoming, friendly, and supportive. Because climate is a psychological construct and perceptions of the given environment may differ depending on the individual and fluctuating circumstances, climates are typically measured in terms of shared perceptions among those who experience it. As Cress (2002), drawing on Tierney (1997), notes, "There is no difference between perception and reality" (p. 391). Rather, the "reality" of climate is rooted in how the environment is constructed and interpreted by its members. Thus, the shared perception of climate may differ depending on the constituency—for example, students of color might perceive the campus climate as "chilly," while white students perceive the same environment to be welcoming and supportive. Campus or classroom climates reflect values, belief systems, norms, ideologies, rituals, and traditions that serve to guide institutional culture. In turn, campus climate and culture are shaped by the broader sociopolitical and economic context such as the local community and geographic region where they are situated (Adelman and Taylor, 2005). Research suggests there are significant relationships (correlative) between climate and students' engagement, achievement, self-efficacy, social and emotional development, and overall quality of their campus life (Adelman and Taylor, 2005).

Hurtado and colleagues have offered considerable scholarly perspectives and research on campus climate and diversity (Hurtado, Carter, and Kardia, 1998; Hurtado, Clayton-Pedersen, Allen, and Milem, 1998; Hurtado, Milem, Clayton-Pedersen, and Walter, 1999). Of particular note is a four-dimensional framework for assessing and describing campus climates as a product of (1) the historical context of the institution and its inclusion or exclusion of various racial and ethnic groups; (2) structural diversity in terms of numerical and proportional representation; (3) psychological factors, including perceptions and attitudes toward particular groups; and (4) behavioral factors characterized by the nature of intergroup relations on campus (Hurtado, Clayton-Pedersen, Allen, and Milem, 1998). Importantly, Hurtado and colleagues reveal the vast majority of approaches to examining climate are often framed from a structural perspective alone, yet when representation of racial and ethnic groups is increased without consideration to the other dimensions, problems are likely to result.

This chapter reviews numerous aspects of institutional climate that have been studied as indicators of gender equity, including classroom experiences and inclusive curricula; campus safety; salary equity; valuation, respect, and collegiality; the double bind; and the "ideal worker" and gender norms that contribute to perceptions that minimize traditionally feminized work (for example, care-giving work).

Classroom Climate

As women increasingly gained access to college classrooms over the twentieth century, it was often assumed they would benefit from an education equal to their male counterparts. Academic women in the United States began to systematically examine classroom experiences of women in coeducational environments during the 1960s women's movement. By introducing the labels "classroom climate" and "chilly climate," Hall and Sandler (1982) gave a name to a problem that had long existed but remained largely invisible. Along with "chilly climate," the terms "gender bias" and "gender discrimination" were also used in the literature to describe classroom environments that disadvantage girls and women. More recently, "chilly climate" has also been employed to describe classroom practices that may disadvantage students of color, gay, lesbian, bisexual and transgendered students, poor students, and students with disabilities regardless of gender (Chism, 1999).

Claims made in the 1982 chilly classroom report emerged from an understanding that classrooms reflect the strengths, weaknesses, and biases of the larger society in which they are situated (Sandler, Silverberg, and Hall, 1996). It is from this vantage point that numerous faculty behaviors, largely unconscious, came to be understood as contributing to classroom environments that disadvantage women. Specific examples include calling on male students more often than women, asking follow-up questions of men and not women, focusing more on a woman's appearance than her accomplishments, paying more attention when men speak, viewing marriage and parental status differently for men and women, and attributing women's achievements to something other than their abilities (Hall and Sandler, 1982; Sandler, Silverberg, and Hall, 1996).

In addition to the work of Sandler and colleagues (Hall and Sandler, 1982; Sandler, Silverberg, and Hall, 1996), studies lending support to claims of climates (both inside and outside of classrooms) that may disadvantage female students in higher education include those by Banks (1988), Brooks (1982), Follet, Andberg, and Hendel (1982), Foster and Foster (1994), Holland and Eisenhart (1992), Rienzi, Allen, Sarmiento, and McMillin (1993), and Rosenfeld and Jarrard (1985). Astin's study of 27,000 college students (1993) concluded that college experiences and environments can "preserve and strengthen, rather than reduce and weaken, stereotypic differences between men and women in behavior, personality, aspirations, and achievement" (p. 406). More recently, building on the work of Pascarella and others (1997), Whitt and others (1999) found undergraduate women experience a climate that "has a negative impact by the end of the first year of college [that] continues and broadens" (p. 175).

Some studies have contested claims of chilly climates in postsecondary classrooms or have reported a more complex picture. For instance, drawing on observational data, Constantinople, Cornelius, and Gray (1988) found that class size and time of the semester were more likely than student or instructor gender to influence students' participation in class (see also, Cornelius, Gray, and Constantinople, 1990). Crawford and MacLeod (1990) found no significant differences between male and female students in their perceptions of classroom climate and concluded that class size is "clearly the variable of most importance to student participation" (p. 120). Based on nearly sixteen thousand responses to the College Student Experiences Questionnaire, Drew and Work (1998) concluded there was "no evidence . . . that women are currently suffering from a chilly classroom climate" (pp. 550, 552). They further asserted, "This is most probably due to the fact that such a climate does not exist extensively in higher education" (p. 552).

Acknowledging "inconsistent and conflicting" findings of the research on classroom climate, Salter's study (2003) examined interactions among learning style, gender, and educational climate and concluded that the perceived fit of classroom experiences may be more related to an interaction of these variables than gender alone. Surveying both male and female students in sex-atypical majors, Serex and Townsend (1999) found these students did not perceive their major field as having a "chilly climate" but did find that both "female and male nursing and education students perceived fewer chilling practices in their major than did female and male accounting and engineering students" (p. 536). The authors concluded that more research is needed to assess whether or not "chilling practices" remain a viable concept in classroom climate research and proposed that future studies drawing on survey data be triangulated with qualitative data, including observations of classrooms and interviews with both faculty and students.

Drawing on both behavioral observations and self-report questionnaires, Brady and Eisler (1999) measured student and faculty perceptions of their college classroom environments and found only borderline statistically significant differences between male and female students' perceptions of classroom environment. Recognizing the discrepancies among research findings related to gender and classroom climate, these researchers suggested that methodological differences may be a contributing factor and proposed that students may be able to accurately identify overt instances of gender bias in classrooms but less able to describe some of the subtle ways in which this bias occurs. For instance, they suggested students may be "more aware of quantitative differences in classroom interaction patterns but less aware of qualitative differences" such as tone of voice and type of instructor feedback (Brady and Eisler, 1999, p. 138).

Findings of chilly classroom environments for women have been corroborated in recent studies. In a study I codirected with Mary Madden (Allan and Madden, 2006), we surveyed nearly four hundred undergraduate women across different fields of study at a public research university and found 25 percent or more reported experiencing behaviors characteristic of chilly classrooms at least "sometimes" (for example, male peers taking over leadership in small group activities [58 percent]; sexually suggestive stories, jokes, or humor [55 percent]; male students taking up more class time than females [41 percent]; males making disparaging remarks about women's behaviors [37 percent]; and men ignoring their ideas or input [28 percent]). Another study based on 403 students enrolled at a community college led researchers to conclude that women found the campus climate to be chillier than men, as did students of color compared with their white counterparts (Morris and Daniel, 2008). Data from these studies indicate that more attention to understanding and preventing chilly classroom behaviors is important as "women's perceptions of college environment can influence their self-efficacy and consequently their success" (Bandura, 1997, cited in Morris and Daniel, 2008, p. 271).

Climate Beyond the Classroom

Outside their college classrooms, students experience campus climate in a myriad of ways. Scholarship on gendered aspects of campus climate for students has examined a range of factors influencing shared perceptions of cocurricular life for women enrolled in postsecondary institutions, including engagement, leadership outside classrooms, campus safety, and romance culture. A synopsis of the research in each of these areas is summarized next.

Student Engagement and Cocurricular Leadership

Adding to the data on the representation or *presence* of women in athletics, student government leadership, and other activities outside the classroom reviewed in the previous chapter, scholars also examine the gendered *experiences* of engagement and cocurricular leadership. The concept of student engagement incorporates two basic concepts: (1) the amount of time and effort students put into studies and other educationally purposeful activities, and (2) how institutions support student engagement through the curriculum, support services, and learning opportunities outside the classroom (Kuh, 2001, 2003; Kuh, Kinzie, Schuh, and Whitt, 2005). In their study of the relationship between gender and student engagement in college, Kinzie and others (n.d.) drew on National Survey of Student Engagement data to examine differences in the type of engagement while in college. More specifically, women were more likely to dedicate time to working hard and serving others, while male students were more likely to report devoting time to interacting with faculty members about ideas, leading the researchers to conclude the differences "illustrate the persistence of gender-related patterns of behavior and learning and warrant further investigation for the differential impact they may have on student learning and success" (p. 20).

In their synthesis of research since the 1990s, Pascarella and Terenzini (2005) summarize findings that clearly indicate differences in the effects of college according to both gender and race. In terms of gender differences and the net effects of college, their review of the literature produced the following conclusions:

Women gain smaller knowledge acquisition benefits from college than men.

In terms of identity development and locus of control, women and men change to about the same extent during college.

Social and political attitudes and values of women and men change about the same degree toward liberal. When the issues involve gender or race, liberal social attitudes are more pronounced among women.

The advantage in occupational status attributable to a bachelor's degree (versus a high school diploma) is about 1.7 times as large for men as for women and twice as large for an associate's degree (pp. 620–621).

In research related to undergraduate leadership, Pascarella and Terenzini (1991) reported that women who served in leadership roles of cocurricular activities were more likely to select careers in male-dominated fields. Astin's research (1993) documented that women involved in sororities were more likely to report increased leadership abilities than women who did not join these groups and that attending a women's college had a positive effect on many leadership outcomes. Women who joined sororities were more likely to be elected to office in college and report increases in their leadership abilities. Whitt's research (1993) on women's colleges revealed that participation in leadership activities was linked to positive intellectual and affective outcomes for women students.

Kezar and Moriarty (2000) examined data from 9,731 students across 352 four-year institutions and found gender and race differences in self-perception of leadership and among the types of experiences that contributed to developing leadership. In terms of gender, both African American and Caucasian men rated themselves higher than women did on growth of leadership abilities, public speaking, and self-confidence during college. Women of both races, however, perceived higher rates of growth in both intellectual and social confidence than did their male counterparts. The findings related to male students' perceptions of their leadership abilities suggest that men students may take better advantage of leadership opportunities in college, or, as the authors point out, the opportunities available to strengthen leadership skills are "a better fit for men or were developed with this population in mind" (p. 65). Involvement in volunteer work for African American men, formal positional leadership (being elected to office) for Caucasian men and African American women, and being active in student organizations for Caucasian women were found to be most helpful in contributing to the development of leadership for each of these subgroups, pointing to the need for student leadership development programs to consider such differences and for ongoing research to further explore these patterns.

Campus Safety

A large body of scholarship and policy work has focused on campus safety, including such topics as alcohol and other drug use, binge drinking, hazing, suicide, gambling, and violence. Traditional-aged college students make up sample populations for the vast majority of campus health and safety studies, and with the growing number of women returning to school in their mid-to late twenties and thirties, it is important to note their experiences may not be fully represented by the extant literature.

Although many health and safety studies provide insight about differences between male and female students related to binge drinking or other issues, the literature on relationship violence and rape has provided the most depth of focus on gender as a central variable in shaping campus culture and climate for students. For instance, in their national study, Koss, Gidycz, and Wisniewski (1987) found the incidence of sexual assault among college women to be thirty-eight per one thousand. Subsequent studies have found that thirty-five per one thousand in a given academic year (6.9-month period) will experience a rape or attempted rape; when this number is projected out over the span of an average college career, 20 to 25 percent of women will experience rape or attempted rape during college (Fisher, Cullen, and Turner, 2000). Despite efforts at prevention, the incidence does not appear to be declining, and research indicates most of these incidents (90 percent) involve an offender known to the woman raped or assaulted (McMahon, 2008). Data compiled by the U.S. Department of Justice reveal that in addition to rape, 13 percent of college women are stalked for sixty days or more during the academic year (Fisher, Cullen, and Turner, 2000).

Sexual assault is often described as the "silent epidemic," in that it remains dramatically underreported. Studies indicate a substantial portion of women who are raped or sexually assaulted do not report the incident (American Association of University Women, 2010; Warshaw, 1994). Although reasons for not reporting sexual assault are wide-ranging and include embarrassment, fear of reprisal, and blaming the victim (Scherer Hawthorne, 2002), a recent investigation by the Center for Public Integrity (2010), found that institutional barriers were the most frequently cited reasons for not reporting an incident. These barriers included issues as administrators who respond to students with disbelief and campus judicial processes that are difficult to understand and navigate. Further, "many students who faced these barriers reported transferring or withdrawing from their college or university while the alleged offenders were almost uniformly unpunished" (American Association of University Women, 2010). In addition to these implications for campus climate, in nearly every case it has been found that college students victimized by sexual assault do not perform at the same academic levels as they did before the incident (American Association of University Women, 2010).

Studies on factors related to sexual assault indicate that alcohol, rape myths, and gender stereotypes increase risk. As well, a "man's acceptance of traditional sex roles, involvement in interpersonal violence, and adversarial attitudes about relationships have also been found to contribute to sexual aggression" (Scherer Hawthorne, 2002, p. 350). In addition to the negative consequences individual women experience as victims of rape, sexual assault, and stalking on campus, women as a group experience the chilling effects of living in an environment where it is estimated nearly thirty-five of every one thousand college women experience attempted or completed rape in a given academic year (Fisher, Cullen, and Turner, 2000). Further, female students also experience chilling effects of sexual and peer harassment on campus, including unwanted and unwelcome verbal, nonverbal, and physical behavior contributing to sexually hostile learning or working environments (Hill and Silva, 2005). Such harassment has "permeated women's academic experiences since their inclusion in postsecondary institutions" (Reichmuth, 2002, p. xx), and recent research confirms these behaviors remain widespread (Hill and Silva, 2005).

According to research conducted by the AAUW Educational Foundation and described in *Drawing the Line* (Hill and Silva, 2005), 62 percent of college women and 61 percent of men report having been sexually harassed at their college or university. Although both female and male students report being targets of sexual harassment, the research indicates that women students report more negative effects: 68 percent of college women compared with 35 percent of college men who experienced sexual harassment report having been "somewhat" or "very upset" by the incidents. Further, female students are more likely to experience physically aggressive forms of sexual harassment such as grabbing. Like sexual assault, sexual harassment is also underreported; 35 percent or more of those experiencing the harassment report they did not tell anyone about it. Nevertheless, 66 percent of college students report knowing someone personally who was the target of harassment (Hill and Silva, 2005).

Women students experience sexual harassment in a number of contexts, including peer, faculty, and administrator relationships. Some studies indicate graduate students tend to experience harassment more from male faculty and instructors than peers (Reichmuth, 2002, p. 102). A 1996 study by the American Psychological Association reported approximately 13 percent of women graduate students had been sexually harassed and that 21 percent avoided classes for fear of sexual harassment. Although most colleges and universities now have formal policies prohibiting both sexual assault and harassment, these statistics underscore that although such efforts are important, they are insufficient for eliminating these behaviors and creating climates free of harassment (Reichmuth, 2002).

Romance Culture
Research related to "romance culture" is another body of work focused primarily on gender and students' experiences of campus climate. Much of the literature in this area emerged from research described by Holland and Eisenhart in their groundbreaking work, *Educated in Romance: Women, Achievement, and College Culture* (1992), in which they share results of their ethnographic study of women undergraduate students enrolled in two colleges, one predominantly

white and one predominantly black, during the early 1980s, with follow-up data collected four years after graduation. Their examination of the experiences of these young women led the researchers to conclude that a major component of campus culture was its organization around romance and attractiveness. Holland and Eisenhart describe practices and social systems that shape a peer culture that places women on the "sexual auction block," where they are constantly exposed to judgments of their worth based on sexual attractiveness. They also found that both academic pursuits and same-sex friendships were pushed aside in favor of romantic relationships with men: in other words, the cultural premium placed on romantic heterosexual relationships "prompted women to prioritize romantic relationships at the expense of academic pursuits and female solidarity" (Gilmartin and Sax, 2002, p. 346). Although some dismiss these assertions as reflecting antiquated attitudes that have shifted dramatically over intervening years, recent scholarship suggests the findings may remain relevant. For example, a 2009 study found many female students consume alcohol based on the assumption that male students will find them more attractive (LaBrie and others, 2009), and in interviews with college women in their senior year, Taylor and Marienau (2008) found nearly half (nine of twenty) "reported they would be marrying their current boyfriend and that this goal took priority in their planning process" (p. 143). Research related to romance culture sheds light on how societal gender patterns related to heterosexual romance continue to influence experiences and sometimes limit the aspirations of women students in higher education.

Climate for Women Staff, Faculty, and Administrators

Because campus climate is shaped by the larger sociopolitical context and underlying values, ideologies, belief systems, and norms of the larger culture, common climate-related themes apply to women in multiple roles on campus regardless of whether they are students, professional staff, or senior leaders. Not surprisingly though, climate-related issues can be somewhat more nuanced for women depending on their role and status in the institution, and positional status can be further compounded by other identity differences like race, social class, and sexual identity. The strength and depth of research relative to women and campus climate varies by issue and constituent group. For instance, although numerous studies have examined climate-related issues affecting women faculty and senior leaders, comparatively few studies are specifically related to professional staff (nonadministrative) and data are lacking related to women in classified staff positions in higher education. The next sections review the literature on work life satisfaction and balance between family and career, especially as these issues relate to faculty.

Work Life Satisfaction

The concept of work life in higher education encompasses a range of dimensions, and the research in this area has grown considerably, especially with regard to faculty. Johnsrud (2002) provides an extensive review of the literature, dating back to Bowen and Schuster's publication of *American Professors: A National Resource Imperiled* (1986) and Scott's publication, *Lords, Squires, and Yeoman: Collegiate Middle Managers and Their Organizations* (1978). In general, according to Johnsrud, research on work life in higher education can be grouped into three categories: (1) studies that work to describe dimensions of work life and explore differences among types of institutions and constituent groups (according to gender, race, and rank); (2) studies that are designed to examine the quality of work life as a predictor of attitudinal outcomes (such as satisfaction); and (3) studies designed to examine aspects of work life and how they may be linked to specific behavioral outcomes like productivity or intent to leave (2002, pp. 380–382).

Hagedorn's proposed framework (2000) to conceptualize and organize the range of factors that can influence work life satisfaction includes (1) motivators and hygienes—job characteristics such as salary, level of achievement, work itself, and recognition; (2) demographics such as gender, race, academic discipline, and institutional type; (3) environmental conditions, including collegiality, relationships with students, and campus culture or climate; and (4) triggers such as a change in one's life or family status, circumstances, or rank. Since the earlier work of Johnsrud and Hagedorn, numerous studies have examined work life satisfaction among faculty. A number of them examine demographic differences and have found stark contrasts between men and women on a number of indicators. For example, a 2004 study by Louise August and Jean Waltman of the Center for the Education of Women at the University of Michigan found the variables in the environmental conditions category (collegiality, campus culture, and climate) were among the most significant predictors of career satisfaction for all faculty women, regardless of rank.

A report by Cathy Trower and Jared Bleak (2004) based on analysis of data gathered from 983 assistant professors at six major research universities found young female professors were less satisfied than young male professors on nineteen of twenty-eight measures. Dissatisfaction with faculty life was attributed to factors that included lack of sufficient time and money for research, unclear expectations about tenure, and lack of support from department chairs. In a 2006 opinion piece published in the *Journal of Women in Educational Leadership*, Misty Schwartz, then an assistant clinical professor of nursing, reflected on aspects of gender and academic life that often serve to dissuade promising women graduate students from pursuing faculty careers:

> *I'm glad no one told me that many women find the academy unappealing, with a chilly environment that can be biased and hostile toward women. I'm glad no one told me that I might suffer from intellectual and social isolation that is brought about by the masculine principles of competition and individualism. I'm glad no one told me that I will have little guidance from my peers due to lack of mentors and that I may be expected to compromise my personal values and beliefs to fit into the white male dominated academic culture. . . . I'm glad no one told me that I would probably report lower satisfaction than white males on relationships with colleagues, professional development, and overall career experience. I'm glad no one told me because I may not be in the position I am in today and now that I am here, I have the opportunity and responsibility to do something about these issues with women in higher education [p. 265].*

Sharing similar sentiments but choosing to abandon her plans for a faculty career in favor of research with a nonprofit environmental organization, Anna Sears, a population biologist from the University of California, Davis, surveyed graduate students in math and science at that institution to determine whether others felt similarly. Her analysis of 258 completed surveys revealed that among graduate students surveyed, "women were much more likely [15 percent] than men [3 percent] to abandon their plans for an academic career. Women cited a clash between a research career and a family, as well as 'disillusionment with academia' because of its 'low pay, political infighting, and harsh competition for money,'" (Wilson, 2004, p. 7). Further, an investigation by Hart and Cress (2008) revealed women faculty were more likely to indicate committee work was a source of stress and reported they were expected to do more service than their male colleagues and were not rewarded for their work.

Earlier studies have revealed that attrition rates for new faculty are two times greater for women than men (Rothblum, 1988). More recent data analyzed from surveys conducted by the Collaborative on Academic Careers in Higher Education (COACHE) have illuminated perspectives of junior faculty members and their satisfaction with work life. Most recently, a COACHE survey of 8,500 pretenure faculty working at ninety-six diverse types of four-year institutions analyzed both gender and racial differences in satisfaction, where culture, climate, and collegiality remain key and persistent problems for minority groups and white women as well. In an effort to tease out which aspects of institutional or departmental culture and climate were particularly problematic and for whom, the survey found that Asian, African American, and Native American faculty were less satisfied than their white and Latino colleagues on a series of questions related to institutional culture, climate, and collegiality. As well, women were less satisfied than men with how they spend their work time and report less satisfaction with research, teaching, and work hours than their male counterparts. When asked about culture and collegiality in general, male and white professors report greater levels of satisfaction.

In addition to documenting perceptions of graduate students and junior faculty relative to the climate for women in the academy, studies have shown similar sentiments shared among more senior-level women. In a 2007 study of women faculty based on interview data, Stout, Staiger, and Jennings found that women "felt demoralized" based on their experiences in the academy (p. 124). More specifically, the accumulation of microinequities experienced throughout their careers led women faculty to question the worth of their position and perceive "the rewards for their hard work to be minimal and unsatisfying (p. 137).

In general research in this area indicates the perceived quality of work life is a key factor in faculty morale and "intent to leave" their current position (Johnsrud and Rosser, 2002). Despite their overall increased representation among faculty, women continue to feel marginalized and devalued (V. J. Rosser, 2004; Valian, 1999), and research indicates these perceptions have consequences for the quality of work life. Clearly, numerous issues contribute to work life satisfaction, but the stress of attempting to balance career and family is an area that is receiving increased attention by researchers.

Family Balance

Among the numerous variables affecting satisfaction with work life, one issue at the foreground of the literature is the challenge associated with balancing family and career demands. Although both men and women choosing to be professionals, partners, and parents face challenges of balancing competing demands, the gendered expectations of family life tend to leave women with careers burdened with the "double day" as a result of the emotional and physical labor involved with caring for children, aging parents, and home as well as the career-related work (Hochschild, 1997). This factor, coupled with the physical demands of pregnancy and motherhood, make challenges of balancing career and family even greater for women.

A body of scholarship relates to work and family in the context of higher education. In general, the research is anchored in personal experience and critiques structures of the academy that have marginalized and excluded women generally and their roles as mothers and partners specifically (Wolf-Wendel and Ward, 2003, 2006b). In describing challenges women faculty face in this regard, scholars have pointed out that current norms of faculty life have emerged from "the history and tradition of an academic life that is male and childless" that contributes to an "ideal worker" norm of one who, "in essence, is married to his work leaving little time for bearing or raising children" (Williams, 2000, cited in Wolf-Wendel and Ward, 2006a, p. 489). "The clockwork of the academic career is also distinctly male. That is, it is built upon men's normative paths and assumes freedom from competing responsibilities such as family" (Ward and Bensimon, 2002, cited in Wolf-Wendel and Ward, 2006a, p. 489). These norms help to explain why many women faculty are far more likely than their male colleagues to be single or have no children (Eddy, 2002; Mason and Goulden, 2004).

A recent study by Mary Ann Mason, Marc Goulden, and Karie Frasch (2009) from the University of California, Berkeley, points to the effects these perceptions have for doctoral students considering faculty careers. In their survey of eighty-three hundred doctoral students across the University of California system, they found 84 percent of women and 74 percent of men were "somewhat or very concerned about the family friendliness of their future employers. Further, only 46 percent of men and 29 percent of women envision jobs in research universities to be somewhat or very family friendly" (Jaschik, 2009). Shifting these perceptions will likely require a sea change. Marcus (2007) notes that experts say longer maternity leaves will not be sufficient. Rather, "it will take significant changes in America's higher education culture so that women no longer suspect—regardless of what the faculty handbook might say—that they'll be seen as weak for taking time off to raise a child" (p. 28).

The concept of "greedy institutions" posited by Coser (1974) to describe the all-consuming commitment of academic work, particularly on the tenure track, has been drawn upon to help explain the elusive balance of work and family for women (Wolf-Wendel and Ward, 2003; Grant, Kennelly, and Ward, 2000). In an investigation of the professional and personal lives of more than six hundred scientists teaching at doctoral-granting departments in U.S. universities, "very few scientists questioned their occupation's demand for an unyielding commitment to science as the center point of their lives" (Grant, Kennelly, and Ward, 2000, p. 67). It has been documented that faculty in the sciences work an average of about fifty hours a week through age sixty-two (Goulden, Frasch, and Mason, 2009).

Arguably, men also feel pressured by all-consuming career expectations. But because women take up the greater share of caregiving in society, it is women who often shoulder a greater burden for this work. The burden is one that can ultimately disadvantage them professionally and take a personal toll as well. For instance, when faculty ages thirty to fifty with children in the University of California system reported on their combined work for career, caregiving, and housework, women averaged one hundred hours a week, compared with eighty-six for men with children (Goulden, Frasch, and Mason, 2009).

These dynamics may help explain why 93 percent of current male college and university presidents are married, compared with only 48 percent of female presidents. As Eddy (2002) explains, "The cultural expectation for the male presidents is that they have a wife at home taking care of the household aspects of life" (p. 501). When a president is female and married to a man, the role of the president's spouse tends to be reconceptualized such that a male partner is assumed to have a career of his own and is not expected to perform the unpaid functions of a president's wife. Yet because the functions typically performed by the female spouse remain to be accomplished, the woman president must assume responsibility for them (Eddy, 2002).

Although challenging, some research on work-family balance lends support to the assertion that the ever-elusive "balance" may be possible for women (Ropers-Huilman, 2000; Ward and Wolf-Wendel, 2004), or at the very least, "the roles of faculty member and mother are not impossible to reconcile" (Ward and Wolf-Wendel, 2008, p. 253). Ward and Wolf-Wendel's extensive research in this area found that "academic women who combine work and family while on the tenure track at research universities can have a positive experience" as children help put the "stress of tenure into a more healthy perspective and . . . women successfully juggle multiple roles by 'satisficing' or doing the best they can in any given situation or role (Wolf-Wendel and Ward, 2006a, p. 492), allowing those who move between both spheres reprieve from the stress inherent in each sphere (Ward and Wolf-Wendel, 2004).

Nevertheless, the stress of balancing the demands of the tenure track and family are underscored by research examining productivity levels of faculty with young children and findings indicating that young children lower the publication output of female academics especially (Stack, 2004, p. 914; June, 2009; Webber and Lee, 2009). It should also be noted that, even when productivity is controlled for, studies confirm that women earn less and advance more slowly than their male counterparts in the academy (Valian, 1999).

Extending the literature in this area, Wolf-Wendel and Ward's research (2006a) analyzes how women faculty perceive the balancing act of work and family differently depending on institutional context. For instance, women faculty with young children on the tenure track at research universities and striving comprehensive campuses perceived their institutions to be less supportive compared with faculty at regional comprehensive universities where teaching and service were emphasized over research and the focused sense of mission of these institutions contributed to an enhanced sense of clarity in tenure requirements, making it somewhat easier to balance competing demands of work and family. Researchers have also found that women faculty with children at community colleges appear to be able to have the most opportunity for balance, though gendered challenges remain (Wolf-Wendel, Ward, and Twombly, 2007).

Leadership

Research on the climate for women campus leaders provides another window through which to examine the status of women. Numerous scholarly investigations about women as academic and administrative leaders (see, for example, Amey and Eddy, 2002; Astin and Leland, 1991; Bornstein, 2008; Glazer-Raymo, 1999; Nidiffer, and Bashaw, 2001; Sagaria, 1988) and work focused on gender, race, and other identity differences in leadership (for example, Bensimon, 1991; Chliwniak, 1997; Eddy and Cox, 2008; Grady, 2002; Jablonski, 1996; Kezar and Moriarty, 2000; Kezar, 2002) have contributed vital perspectives to the rapidly expanding landscape of leadership research and to our understandings of women's status as leaders in higher education. Numerous analyses critique predominant conceptualizations of leadership that can create particular challenges for women leaders in higher education. The next paragraphs summarize scholarship that works to explain why women advance (or do not) to formal positions of leadership and what their experiences are like when they do attain such leadership roles.

Scholars seeking to understand and explain barriers and impediments to career advancement for women administrators illuminate how prevailing and narrow understandings of leadership place women at a disadvantage. "Strongly held cultural beliefs about leaders and leadership are rampant in colleges and universities, often expressed as metaphors. . . . Maintaining such limited definitions and images of leaders leaves women with a narrow band of acceptable behavior as leaders. Women administrators report feelings of marginalization, lack of authenticity, and evidence of cumulative disadvantage when confronted with the choice of professional promotion by adhering to traditional norms and expectations or enacting a more personally genuine construction of leadership" (Amey and Eddy, 2002, p. 484).

Gender discourses permeate the culture, and higher education is not immune from them. For instance, Amey and Twombly's research (1992) revealed language used to describe leadership at community colleges reinforced white male norms of leadership. Although contemporary scholarship in higher education tends to advocate for relational (team, pluralistic, and collaborative) models of leadership and suggests that autonomous, masculine ("great man") perspectives are no longer dominant (Bensimon, Neumann and Birnbaum, 1989; Kezar, Carducci, and Contreras-McGavin, 2006), images of autonomous, masculine approaches to leadership continue to circulate and influence beliefs about leadership that reinforce white male norms (Allan, Gordon, and Iverson, 2006; Eddy and VanDerLinden, 2006; Ford, 2006). The persistence and valorization of these images, despite the critiques of such approaches, can contribute to creating chilly leadership climates for women and for men of color.

Earlier research on women and leadership examined differences between male and female leaders. For instance, some scholarship advanced or tested the idea that women were naturally more "generative" and collaborative in their leadership approaches than men (see, for example, Chliwniak, 1997; Jablonski, 1996). This dichotomized and often essentialist approach was expanded by scholarship that examined how women learn to adapt to masculine organizational norms (Glazer-Raymo, 1999) and how both men and women "learn" to perform gendered versions of leadership that are acquired skills rather than innate or natural to their biological sex. Whether nature or nurture is open to debate; however, Helgesen (1990, 1995) and others who have studied both male and female leaders assert that gender differences in leadership approaches do exist. More specifically, Helgesen (1990, 1995) found that women leaders are more likely to lead their organizations as "webs of inclusion" rather than traditional hierarchies. In so doing, women leaders emphasize process, participation, and devoting time and energy to creating connections between people.

From her in-depth interviews with seven women college presidents, Jablonski (1996) found these women emphasized a generative approach to leadership characterized by empowerment, collaboration, listening to others, and shared decision making. Yet based on data from thirty-five interviews with faculty members from the seven campuses led by these presidents, only two of the seven leaders were described as generative; the remaining five were described in terms characteristic of traditional male models of leadership. Jablonski's analysis proposed that the gap between perceptions of self and others for these women leaders may have been attributable to both organizational structures that did not support the generative approaches and to conflicting expectations on the part of faculty who desired participatory leadership but also wanted a leader to fit their image of a strong and aggressive (masculine) decision maker.

More recent research explores predominant images of leadership and their potential implications for women in higher education, corroborating Jablonski's findings (Allan, Gordon, and Iverson, 2006; Gordon, Iverson, and Allan, 2010). That study examined hundreds of narratives about leadership and leaders in *The Chronicle of Higher Education*. A follow-up investigation in 2009 focused the analysis on gender specifically and found that prevailing images of women leaders were shaped by discourses of femininity, masculinity, professionalism and liberal humanism, and shaped predominant images of women leaders as *caretakers* and *vulnerable leaders* (discourse on femininity), *experts* (discourses on professionalism and masculinity), *relational leaders* (femininity and professionalism discourses), and *social justice leaders* (liberal humanist discourse). It also points out how tensions between dominant constructions of masculinity and femininity continue to place women leaders in a double bind, where they are "damned if they do, and doomed if they don't" (Gordon, Iverson, and Allan, 2010, p. 90). Further, the research revealed that when women leaders act in ways that typify traditional masculinity (being decisive and assertive, for instance), they tend to be described as "noncompliant, disruptive, and controversial." Yet when they behave in ways that typify traditional femininity, they run the risk of being characterized as caregivers first, vulnerable, or unworthy of recognition because they are "keeping a low profile." Accordingly, negative images arising from gendered discourses serve as cultural barriers and are compounded by structural barriers that tend to privilege traditional male-oriented versions of leadership.

Recent research on women college presidents suggests the competing dominant constructions of gender and leadership in which women as caregivers are less likely to be perceived as well suited for leadership may be consequential for women who desire more balance between career and family. "Often subtle discrimination is rooted in gender stereotypes—especially when it comes to the leadership issue. Female candidates are purportedly passed up for promotions based on a conscious or unconscious belief that women do not have what it takes to lead men" (Mason, 2009b).

Alongside Bornstein (2008), Eddy and Cox (2008), and others, Mason (2009a) contends women are often marginalized and thwarted from administrative advancement as the result of an "an accumulation of small and large incidents," including layers of missed networking and career development opportunities resulting from family obligations (like having to leave meetings early to pick up children from day care). These assertions align with Valian's analysis (1999) that "like interest on capital, advantages accrue and that, like interest on debt, disadvantages also accumulate,"(p. 3) ultimately resulting in large disparities in salary, promotion, and prestige for women. The same is not true for men. Rather, research indicates that "marriage and children appear to boost the careers of men and slow or stop those of women" (Mason, 2009b).

Another effect of the double bind for women in leadership roles is the phenomenon of "surplus visibility." "Because the higher they go, the fewer they are, women senior level administrators are ever more exceptional and visible to the point of inviting scrutiny. While visibility can represent an opportunity, living in a 'glass house' with no room for error is more often a problem" (Mason, 2009b).

Overlapping Issues

The majority of climate issues are not isolated to groups of women in particular departments, disciplines, or roles. For instance, women experience sexual harassment as students, faculty members, staff, and administrators. Although certain issues like family care were described in the section on faculty, staff, and administrators, these issues are burdens for many women students as well. Likewise, issues related to campus safety, romance culture, and classroom climate are not isolated to students. It is not uncommon for faculty members to report that the same behaviors that make classrooms "chilly" are present in faculty meetings and other interactions with colleagues. Nevertheless, it is also the case that some climate issues can be more pronounced for some women, depending on differences in disciplinary or departmental environments.

Regardless of a woman's role on a campus, research indicates many of these climate issues can be amplified in male-dominated disciplines and other male-dominated arenas like athletics and fraternities. Largely attributable to the availability of research funds from the National Science Foundation, private foundations, and other government agencies, a substantial body of research has developed around issues particular to women working and studying in the STEM fields (see, for example, Blickenstaff, 2005; Goulden, Frasch, and Mason, 2009; S. V. Rosser, 2004; Stage and Hubbard, 2008). A particularly helpful and current summary of issues and research in this area is provided in *Staying Competitive: Patching America's Leaky Pipeline in the Sciences* (Goulden, Frasch, and Mason, 2009), which highlights several key findings:

Family formation—most importantly marriage and childbirth—accounts for the largest leaks in the pipeline between Ph.D. receipt and acquisition of tenure for women in the sciences.

Research-intensive careers in university settings have a bad reputation with both men and women.

Federal agencies have a shared responsibility with universities in providing adequate family-responsive benefits for America's researchers.

The lock-step structure of academia is unforgiving. Parents, but particularly women, experience significant caregiving responsibilities through age fifty, making it hard for them to keep up with academic career pressures (pp. 2–6).

Further, research has documented that women faculty, particularly in STEM fields, tend to be evaluated more harshly by students in predominantly male disciplines (Basow, 1995).

Another rapidly growing body of scholarship focuses on differences in the category "women" in particular, how women of color experience campus climate. Because many climate issues are linked to power dynamics both overt and subtle, the degree of "chilliness" for women can vary depending on their particular status in institutional prestige hierarchies (for example, clerical staff member or tenured faculty member) and on larger societal prestige hierarchies rooted in other demographic variables like race, socioeconomic status, disability, age, and sexual identity (see, for example, Turner [2003, 2008]; Berry and Mizelle [2006]; Cooper and Stevens [2002]; Zamani [2003]; Hooks [1984]; Collins [1991]; and Ladson-Billings [2000], to name a few. Contributors to Adair and Dahlberg's collection (2003) describe personal and policy challenges for women in higher education who live or have lived in poverty, and McDonough (2002) delineates particular challenges for lesbian women in the academy.

Although important nuances exist relative to particular identity categories (for example, Latina, lesbian, disabled, poor), other common themes are relative to the intersections of race, gender, and other identity categories that have been historically disadvantaged. Experiences of multiple marginality, lived contradictions, and invisibility are some of them. As described by Turner (2002), "situations in which a woman of color might experience marginality are multiplied depending on her marginal status within various contexts. Often it is difficult to tell whether race or gender stereotyping is operating" (p. 77).

Research has documented how tensions resulting from the clash of predominant cultural norms related to both gender and race underpin a number of issues shaping the status of women and campus climate. Images of effective leadership and clashes between the ideal worker norm and balance between work and family are just two such examples. A growing body of work examines the ways in which knowledge production is gendered and raced (Schiebinger, 2004; Harding, 1991, 1993; Smith, 1999) and how taken-for-granted norms around faculty productivity privilege and reward particular kinds of work over others. For instance, Martínez Alemán (2008) describes how "the privileging of research and publication in faculty productivity appraisals further fortifies and reinvigorates the attributes of masculinity in the profession," (p. 143).

The effects of male-dominated networks (old boy networks) have been described by Hoffman (forthcoming) in her research on athletic directors and Sagaria (2002) in her research on administrative hiring decisions at a predominantly white university, where she uncovered how search committee members screened administrative candidates, often unconsciously, through normative, valuative, personal, and debasement filters. More important, these filters were found to be differentially applied depending on the candidate. For instance, the personal filter (where candidates "were screened for their personality, character traits, attitudes, habits, family composition, and sexual orientation") was applied to white women and people of color only and the debasement filter (a form of racism) was applied only to candidates of color (p. 687).

At the same time, these issues represent additional burdens for women who experience multiple marginality, and the situation is often compounded by the frequent failure of white, middle-class, heterosexual, and able-bodied women to acknowledge their own privilege. Thus, a perception often exists among men and women of color that white women cannot be counted on to help dismantle racism and sexism (Turner, 2002). In light of these critiques, a number of white scholars have engaged in research and thinking related to the social construction of whiteness and their own identity privilege (Frankenberg, 1993; McIntosh, 1988). Additionally, some recent scholarship with a focus on differences among women draws on postmodern and poststructural feminism to acknowledging the fluidity of identities that are "in process" and contingent (Braidotti, 1994; West and Fenstermaker, 1995). These approaches are described in more detail in the following chapter.

Salary Equity

Salary equity has been an ongoing concern for women in higher education, and, like data about access and representation of women in the academy, salary data are commonly accepted as indicators of progress toward gender equity and toward improving the status of women in higher education. Although faculty women's salaries are higher on average than they were in previous decades, they are still not equal, overall, to male colleagues at similar ranks. The American

Association of University Professors reports that across all ranks in 2005–06, the average faculty salary for women was only 81 percent of that earned by men.

Pay equity studies in higher education are complex and constantly evolving. Between the 1960s and the late 1990s, more than one hundred studies were conducted to examine gender-based gaps in faculty salaries (Ferree and McQuillan, 1998). Since 2000, numerous studies have examined salary differential by gender and race and explored possible explanations that could account for the gaps. Becker and Toutkoushian (2003) provide an overview of the progress in this line of inquiry and the various perspectives that have shaped current approaches. In general, the vexing question facing researchers has been how much of the salary differential can be reasonably attributed to blatant sexism and how much can be attributed to other factors like rank, productivity, and type of institution—in other words, determining "the unexplained wage gap" (Toutkoushian, 2003, p. 49). More recent studies have also examined correlations between pay differentials and marital status (Toutkoushian, Bellas, and Moore, 2007). Scholarly work in this area has also described relationships between public policy and statistical examinations of gender-based pay disparities (Luna, 2006).

West and Curtis (2006) attribute salary discrepancies to two primary factors: (1) women are more likely to work at institutions with lower salaries, and (2) women are more likely to hold lower-ranking positions. Even when controlling for discipline or field of study, however, women earn 2 to 9 percent less than their male counterparts (Touchton, Musil and Campbell, 2008, p. 21). Recent research by Umbach (2007) explores reasons for the persistent salary gaps based on analysis of nearly eight thousand faculty representing eighty-seven disciplines from 472 four-year colleges and universities. When controlling for discipline and institutional type, Umbach's analysis found a 14 percent pay differential between faculty salaries of men and women. Disciplines with more women have lower average salaries and tend to be more teaching-oriented disciplines. When accounting for other factors that could possibly explain salary gaps such as productivity and teaching loads, a gender-based salary gap of 4 percent remains. Similarly, another large-scale study found that at research universities, when controlling for other factors, a 9 percent salary gap favors men (Porter, Toutkoushian, and Moore, 2008).

Adding to the complexity of research on salary equity, supplemental income is a factor that is often not accounted for in large-scale studies that typically analyze base salaries. Perna's research (2002) on supplemental earnings of faculty members found that "the majority (75 percent) of full-time faculty are supplementing their base institutional salaries with income from other sources and that women are less likely than men to receive most types of supplemental income and when they do receive it, average lower amounts than their male counterparts—even after controlling for differences in human capital and structural characteristics" (p. 52).

Although faculty salaries are important, faculty represent only a fraction of the workers employed by colleges and universities. Do gender-based pay gaps exist among librarians, research associates, admissions counselors, financial aid officers, cooks, coaches, attorneys, grounds crew, accountants, and the myriad of professional, administrative, and operating staff working in postsecondary institutions? Research on these groups has been slim in comparison with the data for faculty. In a study of administrators in more than eight hundred institutions, Pfeffer and Ross (1990) found that women earned less than their male counterparts after controlling for institutional and individual characteristics and job differences (in Toutkoushian, 2003). As well, Johnsrud's research and collaboration with Rosser (2002) has examined gender in relation to midlevel administrators' promotional opportunities and morale. Catalyzed by a request from a university's women's commission, Toutkoushian (2003) examined gender equity in salaries for nonfaculty employed in a postsecondary institution and found that nearly 80 percent of salary differences between men and women across professional and administrative staff and 50 percent among operating staff could be attributed to factors other than gender, including years of experience and the market. As well, the study uncovered discrepancies in pay based on source of funds: more specifically, women whose pay came from soft money sources such as grants were paid 3 to 4 percent less than comparable women who were paid with recurring dollars such as tuition and fees.

Summary

Although important, measuring the attainment of equity by numbers alone is clearly insufficient. Quantitative measures do not typically convey differential quality of educational and work environments for women. Because climate reflects the larger sociopolitical context, including underlying values and norms of the larger culture, and because colleges and universities are microcosms of the larger society, common climate-related themes occur for women in multiple roles on campus regardless of whether they are students, professional staff, or senior leaders. Scholars contend the manner in which colleges and universities are organized, the way they conduct business, and what counts as legitimate knowledge all privilege masculinity and masculine approaches. Thus, it stands to reason that women, who are often considered inherently more feminine than male counterparts, are likely to encounter barriers, challenges, and tensions in such environments.

This chapter reviewed some of the ways in which these challenges manifest for women in higher education. For women students, classroom climates, men's violence, harassment, and romance culture remain climate-related problems. For faculty, staff, and senior administrators, challenges related to the balance between work and family, the "ideal worker norm," conceptualizations of leadership, occupational segregation, and salary inequity are also climate-related issues. These issues are compounded for women of color, first-generation women, lesbian, and disabled women, who must also navigate the climate-related challenges that emerge from workplaces and learning environments that privilege white, middle-class, able-bodied, and heterosexual norms.

Women's status in higher education is obviously more complex than simply a measure of parity. Assessing the attainment of equity by numbers alone does not account for inequitable experiences, as gender-based climate-related issues continue to disadvantage women by draining their energy and inhibiting their full potential. Expanded understandings of equity (those that incorporate campus climate) call for expanded thinking and strategy development beyond increasing the numbers of women in the pipeline (White, 2005).

A number of feminist lenses are evident in the framing of research questions and discussions of climate-related issues described in this chapter. For example, salary equity studies are motivated by questions about the extent to which sex or gender plays a role in pay disparities between men and women. Although not all research on this topic is expressly feminist, salary equity studies taking a feminist approach are best described as "liberal feminist" because of the focus on uncovering inequality and redressing it through formal mechanisms (administrative processes) in the organization.

The influence of radical feminism can be seen in studies that foreground how women's experiences in higher education are impeded by sexism, male control of higher education, and patriarchal norms and practices. Studies examining how women may be disadvantaged by masculine norms of communication, romance culture, sexual harassment, and threat of sexual violence on campus are examples of investigations conceptualized through a radical feminist lens. Multicultural and sometimes global lenses are also evident in some of the literature that notes "multiple marginality" for women of color in the context of institutions where white, Eurocentric, and patriarchal norms have been predominant.

Alongside these studies, psychological and care-focused feminist lenses have shaped approaches to climate-related studies. For example, studies related to the quality of work life highlight ways in which the important care-focused work of social reproduction is devalued for both women and men who are seeking to balance professional and family-related work and fulfillment. In addition, psychological feminist and radical-cultural lenses are noted in those investigations seeking to highlight the need and value of practices typically understood as inherently feminine such as collaborative and inclusive approaches to leadership and consensus-based decision making. Some of the climate literature also reflects postmodern and poststructural feminist lenses that emphasize how the performance of gender and other dominant discourses (for example, professionalism) shape particular realities, including women's status in higher education.

The next chapter reviews and analyzes predominant change strategies designed to enhance women's status in higher education. The focus shifts from describing women's status and continuing barriers to reviewing the literature on change-making strategies, including activism, policy, mentoring, institutional infrastructures, leadership, organizational norms and practices, and curriculum transformation. In the chapter, feminist frames of analysis are drawn upon to illuminate some of the nuances and potential implications for practice in each strategy.

Advancing Women's Status: Analyzing Predominant Change Strategies

A S SET FORTH IN THE SECOND CHAPTER, multiple lenses of feminist theory have evolved over time in response to a central question: How do we eliminate sex or gender inequity? More recently, this question has been broadened to acknowledge and incorporate the fluidity of identity formations and identity-based oppression such as racism and homophobia. As such, feminist theories provide valuable lenses for anyone committed to understanding equity issues. Although a few exceptions exist, however, scholarly articles or committee reports seldom articulate the feminist frame(s) in which their perspectives are grounded. In fact, as Hart's analysis (2006) reveals, research that is explicitly feminist is underrepresented in mainstream higher education academic journals. In her examination of three key journals in the field (*Journal of Higher Education, Review of Higher Education,* and *Research in Higher Education*) between 1990 and 2002, she found fewer than ten articles to be explicitly grounded in feminist research. Despite the relative absence of research that articulates feminist lenses in use, a growing number of researchers in higher education describe their research as feminist and engage in investigations related to gender equity and women's status. In summarizing the implications of their findings, these researchers typically suggest strategies to accelerate the pace of change. Recommendations for advancing the status of women are also found in unpublished committee and task force reports available from college and university Web sites.

In their chapter, "Improving Gender Equity in Postsecondary Education," Cooper and others (cited in Klein and others, 2007) provide a helpful overview of predominant change strategies employed to advance women's status in higher education at the turn of the twenty-first century. As well, numerous articles and edited collections provide in-depth examinations of particular problems and suggested remedies (see, for example, Dean, Bracken, and Allen, 2009). This chapter builds on and extends these other reports by making more explicit connections between feminist theories and predominant approaches to advancing equity in the context of higher education.

Organizing Schemes

The reductive nature of any categorizing scheme can obscure underlying complexity. The potential damage in oversimplification can be seen when claims of gender equity based on aggregate data alone fail to account for nuances related to women's location in the prestige hierarchies or differential treatment based on gender. Oversimplification is also problematic when the range of issues and differences among women resulting from race, social class, and other identity formations is collapsed into the category "women's issues" and framed by those with the most privilege in a particular context.

Exhibit 2 displays women's status indicators in higher education, with a few caveats. First it should be noted that a particular change strategy, like policy development, can cut across multiple feminist frames. Also, it is important to recognize the degree to which some barriers to success, like faculty tenure processes for instance, may differ by institutional type and discipline. Most of the identified barriers or problems are common to all institutional types such as the gender segregation of disciplines as in the "feminized fields" of nursing, education, and social work and the male-dominated fields in the physical sciences and engineering, and the balancing acts between work and family. Some problems, however, may be more relevant to a particular type of institution such as the predominant role of externally funded research at doctoral-granting institutions.

Exhibit 2 compares differences among key feminist frames and their implications for enhancing women's status in higher education. It distinguishes between feminist frames that are highlighted by the underlying problems understood to manifest in the context of higher education. In other words, as reviewed in the second chapter, differences in approaches to enhancing

EXHIBIT 2

Women's Status Indicators in Higher Education: Problems and Change Strategies in Multiple Feminist Frames

FRAME	PROBLEM	MANIFESTATION in higher education	GOAL for change	EXAMPLE STRATEGIES
Liberal	Gender inequality	Discrimination in admissions, hiring, or promotion	Equality of opportunity	Antidiscrimination policies
		Gender segregation		Improve: Recruitment Mentoring Professional Development
		Not enough women in pool		Commissions Task forces Focus on civility Affirmative Action
		Not enough women in pipeline		
Radical	Patriarchy	Male control of higher education and hence women who participate in it	Dismantle patriarchy	Women's centers Women's colleges Women's studies Women across the Curriculum Grants for research on women
		Hierarchies that privilege masculine norms, standards, structures, processes		
Socialist	Privileging corporate and industrial sectors	Marketplace values	Dismantle mutually reinforcing systems of capitalism and patriarchy	Recognize and develop alternatives to capitalist and marketplace-driven academia
		Corporatization		Flatten hierarchies
		Capitalism and patriarchy are inextricably linked; therefore, the marketplace model inevitably advantages men more than women		Job sharing Cooperatives Unions
		Curricula to produce workers		Collaborative leadership and learning

(Continued)

EXHIBIT 2 (Continued)

FRAME	PROBLEM	MANIFESTATION in higher education	GOAL for change	EXAMPLE STRATEGIES
Multicultural/Global, and Postcolonial	Patriarchy, Racism, and Imperialism	Imperialist and Eurocentric structures and practices advantage whites and men. A focus on patriarchy alone is insufficient	Dismantle mutually reinforcing systems of patriarchy, racism, and imperialism	Draw on similar strategies of other frames with intersectionality as an added lens for developing more inclusive approaches
				Implement pedagogies that help dismantle racism, sexism, and other forms of identity oppression
			Value identity differences	Value indigenous ways of knowing
Ecofeminist	Patriarchy is linked with domination of nature	Logic of domination undergirds structures and practices in higher education and results in lack of reverence for Earth and nonhuman life	Transform knowledge and practice	Nurture alternative programs and practices that affirm and value women, nature, and all living things
			Change power-over . approaches	Shift to more Earth-centered approaches like sustainability
		Manifested in the privileging of efficiency and progress at expense of women and the Earth	Dismantle patriarchal tructures that support systems of domination	

| Psychological (Care-focused) | Devaluing the feminine | Problems exist because male domination has failed to acknowledge the value in women's innate strengths to build connections and seek collaboration and consensus

Relatedly, problems also exist because of gender stereotypes that advantage men in structures and processes that privilege masculine qualities over feminine | Feminine is valued as highly as the masculine | Value women's ways of leadership, teaching, learning, and research
Promote connectedness and connected knowing
Create more collaborative team approaches and inclusive decision-making processes |
| Postmodern Poststructural and Third Wave | Regimes of truth | Dominant discourses sustain assumptions that support patriarchy, capitalism, heterosexism, racism, and other make imperialist and other practices of domination appear "natural"

Discriminatory practices are slow to change because change strategies are formulated within dominant discourses | Scholarship provides a means of dismantling regimes of truth

Produce knowledge and practices that challenge stability of "the autonomous subject" and "truths" | Identify dominant discourses shaping strategies and consider unintended consequences
Promote alternative discourses as ways of making meaning
Promote ways of knowing, learning, and working that allow for fluidity, ambiguity and contradiction |

Source: Tong, 2009.

women's status reflect divergent views about the nature of inequity. For example, if the root problem is understood through the lens of gender inequality primarily (liberal feminism), the proposed remedies differ dramatically from remedies conceived through the lens of socialist feminism. Similarly, although liberal and radical strands of feminist thought share in valuing women and striving to enhance their status, the central focus on justice, equality, and fairness for liberal feminists reflects the predominant view that institutions are flawed but can be fixed through improved institutional mechanisms like better policies and enforcement of those policies to achieve equality of opportunity. In contrast, the root problem for radical feminists is the patriarchal nature of the institution itself (not simply flawed practices or policies). Thus, when applied to the context of higher education, the central focus for radical feminists is dismantling patriarchal attitudes, structures, and practices supporting the enterprise of higher education and its institutions.

Although the academy is not necessarily the central focus of any of these schools of thought, as a microcosm of society with great potential to shape social change it is often a key venue of and for feminist theorizing. With this backdrop in mind, an overview of predominant strategies most commonly employed to enhance women's status in higher education follows.

Enhancing Gender Equity

Strategies to promote gender equity and elevate women's status are numerous, and an in-depth examination of each is beyond the scope of this monograph. A review of the predominant types of strategies and research related to them is provided in this chapter, however. Strategies are provisionally organized according to the following themes: (1) activism, organizing, and women's networking; (2) policy-focused strategies; (3) mentoring; (4) augmenting institutional infrastructures; (5) leadership development; (6) altering organizational norms and practices; and (7) curriculum transformation, including women's studies, feminist epistemology, and women-focused research centers.

A review of predominant change strategies reveals interconnections between the categories of access, representation, and campus climate. For instance, Title IX policy and its enforcement were developed to ameliorate discriminatory practices and environments inhibiting equality of education opportunities for girls and women. So although Title IX might be considered a strategy to promote access and representation primarily, it is also a mechanism for improving campus climates, assuming that increased participation of women in higher education will in turn yield more hospitable campus climates. The vast majority of strategies included in this chapter are not necessarily new in the context of higher education. A brief overview of each is sufficient to describe them and illustrate the feminist frames predominant in shaping the strategy and/or scholarship related to it.

Activism, Organizing, and Networking

Most if not all strategies employed to advance women's status in higher education have emerged from women's formal and informal (grassroots) activism. To the extent this activism focuses on foregrounding or advancing the principles of (1) acknowledging women's contributions to the world; (2) acknowledging that sex and gender inequity exists; and (3) working to change sex and gender inequity, the activism can be understood as feminist in nature. Often behind the scenes, feminist activism in higher education, like other arenas, employs both formal mechanisms (policy, task forces, commissions) and grassroots approaches (networking) and has served as a backdrop to policy initiatives, formal changes to the university infrastructure; efforts to shift norms and cultural values; development of women's centers and women-focused curricula and pedagogies; and funding of research by and about women.

Formal mechanisms of feminist activism in higher education are typically conceptualized in the reform-oriented liberal feminist frame with a focus on justice, rights, and fairness where existing college and university structures and processes are employed as a means of change (Glazer-Raymo, 1999). As depicted in Exhibits 1 and 2, some examples of predominant approaches conceptualized in a liberal feminist frame include policy initiatives, professional development programs, mentoring, task forces, and commissions on the status of women. Often precariously situated and at times critiqued as a diversion, policy-focused groups like women's commissions are formulated in the formal structures of the university (they are often "the president's commission on the status of women"). Yet at the same time, they challenge formal structures as they gather data and develop recommendations designed to dismantle discriminatory policies and practices of the institution (Allan, 2003, 2008).

In contrast to formal types of organizing and activism among women in higher education, grassroots activism occurs when individuals without formal positions of authority are interested in and pursue organizational changes that often challenge the status quo of the institution. Grassroots leadership is defined in social movement literature as "the stimulation of social change or the challenge of the status quo by those who lack formal authority, delegated power, or institutionalized methods for doing so" (Wilson, 1973, p. 32). Unlike formal activist mechanisms, the institution or its formal leadership does not officially sanction grassroots approaches. Grassroots feminist activism occurs across constituencies and manifests in a range of ways. Grassroots activism is often linked to formal activism by virtue of the issues and people involved. Grassroots activism is more likely to be conceptualized from perspectives that depart from the traditional liberal feminist approaches. When conceptualized in a radical frame, feminist activism focuses on resisting and uprooting patriarchal thinking and practices that oppress women. That is, radical feminists in the academy are more likely to prioritize issues related to strengthening women-focused programs, centers, and knowledge and helping women gain power through control of their bodies, including their sexuality and reproduction. Examples of these types of feminist activism can be seen in Take Back the Night marches protesting sexual violence on campus and feminist faculty who gather informally to support each other's work and to advance scholarship by and about women.

A number of activist, organizing, and networking strategies to enhance the status of women in higher education extend beyond a single institution and incorporate both formal and grassroots activism. An example is the *Women in Higher Education* (WHE) newsletter. Nearing its twentieth year of publication, the monthly, independent, practitioners news journal (both print and online) with a readership of approximately twelve thousand per month (M. D. Wenniger, personal communication, May 7, 2010) is designed to help women understand how gender affects their success in the male-dominated world of higher education and "to enlighten, encourage, empower, and enrage women on campus by sharing problems and solutions" *(Women in Higher Education,* 2010).

The WHE newsletter summarizes recent scholarship, policy, and news briefs related to women and gender equity; features interviews with women leaders and researchers studying women's status; and includes a section called "career connections" where readers can peruse announcements for college and university job openings. Although the newsletter focuses on many formal strategies for advancing women's status and describes its primary goal as seeking to "increase the number of women in campus leadership" *(Women in Higher Education,* 2010), the strategy itself can be characterized as grassroots in nature as it is independently produced (not affiliated with any college or university) and was "started when the editor received a small inheritance from a great aunt who was a milliner in the 1920s, and who would have been described today as a radical feminist" *(Women in Higher Education,* 2010).

An example of a more formal mechanism of women's organizing and networking across postsecondary institutions is the Program on the Status and Education of Women, established by Bernice (Bunny) Sandler in 1970. An arm of the Association of American Colleges and Universities (AACU), the program continues to provide support to postsecondary women faculty, administrators, and students through programs and publications, including *Campus Women Lead, On Campus with Women* (a free online newsletter), and a series of reports on women of color in the academy (Association of American Colleges and Universities, 2010). Similarly, the Office of Women in Higher Education, initiated in 1973 with the American Council on Education, continues to be a key source of information about women and leadership roles in higher education by hosting forums and summits (such as the Women of Color Summit in 2008) with a focus on leadership (American Council on Education, Office of Women in Higher Education, 2010). The Committee on Women in the Academic Profession (Committee W) of the American Association of University Professors is another formal group established to formulate policy statements and provide resources and reports relative to women faculty, including such issues as pay equity, work and family balance, sexual harassment, and discrimination. Numerous other formally organized groups exist, many of which began as grassroots initiatives but currently continue as formal offices, programs, or committees of established professional associations, collective bargaining groups, and policy-oriented councils and associations.

A powerful example of activist efforts in a single institution is the work by Radcliffe alumnae to promote gender equity at Harvard University over the past two decades. Catalyzed in 1988 at the reunion of the Radcliffe class of 1953 where formal discussion revolved around the question "Is Harvard as sexist today as it was when we were students?" an ad hoc group and subsequent steering committees, including the class of 1958 alumnae, focused on equity of women at Harvard. After assessing the status and determining the climate for women at Harvard was uneven and hostile in some places, the alumnae networks took it on themselves to influence change, noting that unlike other stakeholders, alumnae are in the unique position of being able to "raise a ruckus without fear of repercussions" and characterizing themselves as "pesky little gnats that wouldn't go away" (S. G. Cook, 2008, p. 1). For instance, one of the first strategies the group employed was initiating a not-for-profit organization called the Committee for the Equality of Women at Harvard, recruiting alumnae members and donations to support their efforts. When Harvard administrators showed "little interest" in their mission, the committee decided to hold its $1.6 million in contributions in escrow until "Harvard committed to increasing opportunities for women scholars" (S. G. Cook, 2008, p. 2). Other initiatives of the alumnae group included producing comprehensive reports on the status of women at Harvard, establishing junior fellowships for women faculty, donating $75,000 to start a formal mentoring program for women faculty, supporting campaigns to combat sexual harassment, and opening a campus women's center (S. G. Cook, 2008). In describing the experience of their activism, Radcliffe alumnae reported that progress felt "glacial" but they were buoyed by "the joy of making common cause with women. They fortified each other. They built friendships and had energizing conversations" (S. G. Cook, 2008, p. 2).

Policy

Public policy initiatives (such as federal legislation) have been a cornerstone of efforts to advance women's status in society and in the context of higher education. Throughout the history of U.S. higher education, external policies have shaped a vast array of opportunities and experiences for women working and studying in postsecondary institutions, including student admissions, financial aid, faculty recruitment, compensation, and promotion (see Exhibit 3).

Conceptualized in a liberal feminist frame, public policy initiatives with a direct impact on women's participation in U.S. education include the Nineteenth Amendment (suffrage) passed in 1920 and a series of policy initiatives passed in the 1960s and 1970s reviewed in the first chapter. An extensive historical account of sociopolitical forces shaping U.S. women's movements since 1960 is provided in Davis (1999), which details complexities inherent in the passage of many legislative landmarks, including those with direct implications for higher education like the Equal Pay Act and Title IX. In *Women and Public Policy: A Revolution in Progress*, Conway, Ahern, and Steuernagel (1999) provide a concise summary of policy initiatives and challenges associated with their implementation. From a global feminist perspective, Stromquist (2007) provides a helpful overview of educational policy initiatives related to gender equity.

Specific to higher education, Adair and colleagues (2002) provide helpful reviews of key policy initiatives and legal issues in Martínez Alemán and Renn's *Women in Higher Education: An Encyclopedia*. Glazer-Raymo (1999, 2007, 2008b) has written extensively about public and institutional policies shaping women's status in higher education. Her detailed examinations of policy mechanisms include analyses of affirmative action and Title IX. More recently, her analysis of forces shaping public policy draws attention to the "ungendering" of equity policies (2007, 2008a) evidenced by federal strategies of "threatened reversals of anti-bias and affirmative action statutes and regulations." In light of these troubling trends, Glazer-Raymo (2007) points to the need to "reaffirm a women's rights agenda" (p. 174).

Few would argue that women in higher education have benefited and continue to benefit greatly from the implementation and enforcement of antidiscrimination and equal opportunity policy initiatives. These initiatives have had a particularly positive impact for white women, especially in the areas of access and representation as students and faculty, increased participation in athletics among undergraduate women, and the improvement of campus climate as a result of institutional policies related to sexual harassment developed to comply with Title VII and Title IX. Taken together, gender equality policies have dramatically shifted women's access to and participation in higher

EXHIBIT 3

Key Policy Initiatives Shaping Women's Status in Higher Education

Date	Policy	Focus
1963	Equal Pay Act Amendment to the Fair Labor Standards Act	Prohibited employers from discriminating in payment of wages based on sex among those performing essentially on equal work jobs requiring equal skill, effort, and responsibility under similar working conditions.
1964	Civil Rights Act	Among other provisions, prohibited employment discrimination by programs and activities receiving federal funding based on race, religion, sex, or national origin in employment (did not include sex discrimination in educational programs).
1967	Executive Order 11246, as amended by President L. Johnson	Extended equal employment/affirmative action requirements of federal contractors to women.
1972	Title IX of the Education Amendments of 1972	Prohibits sex discrimination in educational programs and activities receiving federal funds.
	Amendment to Equal Pay Act	Extended coverage to academic personnel.
1974	Women's Educational Equity Act	Created series of programs to promote educational equity.
1975	Public Health Services Act	Prohibited gender discrimination in admission of students to federally funded health services training programs.
1976	Vocational Education Act Amendment	Required states receiving federal funding for vocational programs to reduce barriers caused by gender bias.

(Continued)

EXHIBIT 3 *(Continued)*

Date	Policy	Focus
1978	Pregnancy Discrimination Act	Made it illegal to fire or otherwise discriminate against women because they are pregnant.
1984	*Grove City v. Bell,* 465 U.S. 555 (1984)	Supreme Court ruling limited civil rights laws applying to federal aid recipients only to the specific program directly receiving the aid (financial aid office rather than the full institution).
1987/ 1988	Civil Rights Restoration Act	Clarified Congress's intent to apply laws prohibiting discrimination by recipients of federal funds and their subcontractors to include all programs and activities of the organization—reversing effects of *Grove City* ruling.
1993	Family and Medical Leave Act	Allowed up to twelve weeks unpaid time off of job to recover from illness, care for new child, or ill family members without penalty of losing job.

education, compared with the days when it was legal to refuse admission to women because they were female. Nevertheless, problems remain, including threats to these gains through unenforced agency regulations, court decisions, and public perception that gender equity has been achieved, rendering relevant laws and policies obsolete (Glazer-Raymo, 2008a). Further, the fact that extant policies have not yet resolved the problems related to inequitable representation of and inhospitable climates for women serves as evidence of the need to strengthen what exists rather than allow further erosion (Glazer Raymo, 2007, 2008a). Relatedly, some feminist scholars have argued that traditional modes of policy and policy analysis carry inherent masculine and white biases, limiting their effectiveness altogether (Bacchi, 1999; Bensimon and Marshall, 1997; Pillow, 2003).

Calling for an expansion of predominant frameworks of policy analysis in the context of higher education, Bensimon and Marshall (1997, 2000, 2003) argue for the use of feminist and critical policy perspectives. Recent scholarship from both critical and poststructural feminist perspectives suggests established methods of policy analysis fall short because they typically proceed from an acceptance of policy problems and tend not to analyze the assumptions undergirding the articulation of those problems (Bacchi, 1999; Ball, 1990, 1994; Blackmore, 1999; Marshall, 1999, 2000; Pillow, 1997, 2003; Scheurich, 1994; Stone, 2002). For example, Hawkesworth (1988, 1994) surveys feminist policy studies and points out that such approaches examine the "seldom scrutinized beliefs concerning the nature of facts and values, the powers of reason, the structure of science, and the possibilities for scientific knowledge—beliefs so widely accepted by practitioners in the field that they are no longer perceived as issues" (1988, p. 2). Allan, Iverson, and Ropers-Huilman's collection (2010) highlights research about policy-related issues in higher education through the lens of feminist poststructuralism. For instance, Hart and Hubbard (2010) found that policies intended to support low-income students had the unintended consequence of reinforcing status hierarchies linked to social class.

In sum, contemporary feminist policy perspectives foreground power dynamics related to gender and other identity categories such as race, sexual identity, and social class and examine how they are implicated in policy (see, for example, Blackmore, 1999; Collins, 1991; Fraser, 1989; Fraser and Gordon, 1994; Hawkesworth, 1994; Pillow, 2003; Smith, 1990; Williams, 1991, 1997; Winston and Bane, 1993). Feminist policy analysis has historically emphasized ways in which policy produces uneven effects for men and women. Further, feminist policy analysts in general, and especially those from poststructural perspectives, work to illuminate ways in which power operates through policy by drawing attention to hidden assumptions or policy silences and unintended consequences of policy practices (Allan, 2003, 2008; Bacchi, 1999; Blackmore, 1999; De Castell and Bryson, 1997; Fine, 1988; Pillow, 1997, 2003; Stone, 2002). For example, my research on women's commission policy documents reveals that policy efforts to enhance women's representation in male-dominated arenas of the institution cast women in the position of supplicants or "outsiders" petitioning to enter male domains (for example, by hiring more women; Allan, 2008). In contrast, more recent policy-related recommendations in postsecondary institutions focus more on the deficiencies in the environment that are not conducive to a balance between work and family for either women or men and hence impede work life satisfaction for many.

Mentoring

Across time and venue, recommendations to advance the status of women on campuses abound with recommendations for enhanced mentoring and professional development for women across nearly all constituent groups, especially faculty and administrators (Allan, 2008; Dean, 2009). Mentoring and professional development are typically suggested as promising means of increasing women's access to and participation in arenas where they are underrepresented. Mentoring is promoted as a means of helping women enhance their qualifications like faculty publication records and external funding successes (Dean, 2009). It is also argued that mentoring and targeted professional development can help resolve the pipeline and glass ceiling challenges, especially in the STEM fields and senior leadership (Dean, 2009; S. V. Rosser, 2004). Despite predominance as an accepted strategy, feminists themselves often question the merits of such programs. For instance, it can be argued that by placing the burden on women to seek mentoring or on institutions to provide mentoring for women, such programs may unintentionally frame inequity as an outcome of women's deficiency rather than an outcome of structural or institutional barriers that impede their advancement despite having the requisite qualifications.

In general, a mentor is someone who provides guidance, support, knowledge, and opportunities for a time period deemed helpful to the protégé, with such assistance generally occurring during a time of transition (Wasburn, 2007). More specifically, mentors help to "professionally socialize protégés in the customs, demands, and expectations of organizational and professional cultures" and serve as resources, role models, and opportunity makers (Dean, 2009, p. 130). Numerous scholars consider mentoring vital to career advancement for women and lack of mentoring to be a barrier to their advancement.

Mentoring is most often viewed as an informal process where mentors and protégés come together spontaneously. Seeing the potential value in these kinds of relationships, however, mentoring programs have been instituted in postsecondary institutions. Although formal mentoring programs—those where a third party catalyzes or organizes the mentoring relationship—have been implemented, some evidence suggests they are less effective than informal or spontaneous mentoring relationships (Wasburn, 2007).

Formally organized mentoring programs generally take one of several approaches, including grooming, networking, and strategic collaboration (Wasburn, 2007). Conceptualized in a liberal feminist frame, "grooming mentoring," the most common form, involves a dyadic relationship between a mentor and a protégé and is fraught with potential difficulties because to a large extent, the success of the grooming approach relies largely on the personalities of those involved. Further, grooming types of mentoring approaches have been critiqued for reinscribing hierarchical power dynamics (Altman, 2007; McGuire and Reger, 2003; Wasburn, 2007). In contrast, peer or networking mentoring is conceptualized as a nonhierarchical arrangement with a focus on community building, which may imply more radical and socialist feminist influences. For example, McGuire and Reger (2003) describe a model of feminist comentoring that "challenges masculinist values of hierarchy [and] competition and fosters an equal balance of power between participants while integrating emotion and valuing familial and personal needs" (p. 54). From a poststructural perspective, Iverson (2005, 2007), recommends chaotic mentoring relationships as a means of promoting mentoring that disrupts traditional hierarchical models and holds potential to make alternative discourses more visible, thereby disrupting dominant and entrenched male-oriented conceptualizations of leadership.

Although numerous advocates of gender equity highlight the value of learning from mentors and role models, Valian's research (1999) drawing on the social psychology of gender schemas suggests caution with regard to some types of mentoring. In particular, she contends that role models (the kind of mentoring most reflected by the grooming model) as a means of promoting equitable practices will be ineffective because most figures (women who have achieved high levels of influence and positional power) who are put forth for women to emulate are exceptional cases, as they typically achieved success, not only by merit, but also through other forms of social and material capital.

As well, she asserts that this type of mentoring can send a message that women at lower levels of the organizational hierarchy simply need to "try harder" and do more of the right things so they too will advance. Although role models to spur aspirations may be valuable, the emphasis on these kinds of remedies tends to eclipse structural and dispositional barriers; Valian contends that "women should of course strive for excellence and persevere in the face of failure. But their individual efforts cannot undo the gender schemas that stand in their way" (1999, p. 330).

Scholarship on mentoring also reveals that most formalized programs are designed for those in the early stages of their career. In the case of faculty, however, mentoring may be equally important for women who are later in their careers. For instance, posttenure mentoring may help to rectify the problem of "stalled out" careers for women who plateau at the associate professor level.

Leadership

Related to the goals of mentoring, increasing the numbers of women in the administrative and executive leadership of institutions remains a key goal toward enhancing women's status in higher education. Support for initiatives designed to accomplish this goal emerge from several feminist frames. A liberal feminist frame argues that simply increasing the representation of women in such positions marks progress toward equality of opportunity. Further, when considered from the lens of psychological feminism, it is assumed most women will take different approaches to leadership. For instance, it is not uncommon to hear women described as naturally more collaborative than their male counterparts. Given this premise, it is argued that increasing the representation of women in leadership roles will in turn shift cultural norms and promote more hospitable climates. A related and important outcome of these and multicultural feminist perspectives is that increasing numbers of diverse women in leadership roles will also help enhance aspirations of girls and women who do not currently see themselves reflected in the leadership share.

Mentoring and professional development are considered key strategies for increasing the numbers of women in senior leadership. According to research examining career advancement in higher education, a mentor's tutoring and advocacy can be a valuable asset for career mobility (Dean, 2009; Sagaria and

Rychener, 2002) and can help protégés build networking skills. As more institutions employ private search firms to assist them in hiring senior administrators, networks have become increasingly vital for those aspiring to executive roles. These firms increasingly rely on referrals and informal networks to identify and recommend candidates. For women and men of color, these networks may be more of a liability than for white men, who are more likely to belong to the networks of those making hiring decisions (Sagaria and Rychener, 2002).

Leadership and professional development programs often include one-to-one mentoring as a component but are also focused on building networks and skills needed to provide aspiring leaders with requisite qualifications and experience. Some programs are housed in a single institution or state system of higher education, while others draw from a national audience. Some of the most widely recognized leadership development opportunities for women seeking executive roles in higher education include Bryn Mawr's Higher Education Resource Services (HERS), focused on improving the status of women in middle and executive levels of higher education administration; the American Council on Education's fellows program; the Harvard Graduate School of Education's Management Development Program; and the American Association of State Colleges and Universities's Millennium Leadership Initiative (designed specifically to strengthen preparation of those traditionally underrepresented in executive leadership roles; Turner and Kappes, 2009).

Turner and Kappes (2009) identify twenty-one institutes or programs that provide training or development for individuals aspiring to leadership positions in postsecondary institutions. Four of them are national programs specifically focused on women: HERS, the Center for Women and Leadership Faculty Fellows at Loyola University in Chicago, the Alice Manicur Women's Symposium sponsored by NASPA (Student Affairs Administrators in Higher Education), and the National Institute for Leadership Development. The National Hispana Leadership Institute is the only program focused on women of color (Turner and Kappes, 2009, pp. 173–180). The cost and time commitment involved in such programs range widely, reflecting differences in scope and prestige. For example, the ACE Fellows program involves a year-long placement with a program fee of $7,500 plus a $14,000 professional development budget shared by the nominating institution. In contrast, the NASPA program involves a $625 fee for a one-week full-time commitment (Turner and Kappes, 2009).

Leadership development programs are commonly believed to be an important mechanism for improving women's status in higher education. For example, over the first forty years of the ACE Fellows program (serving approximately thirty-five individuals per year), more than three hundred fellows have become chief executive officers, one thousand have served as provosts or vice presidents, and more than eleven hundred have served as deans (American Council on Education, 2005). Yet, less than 5 percent of those participants were women of color (Turner and Kappes, 2009). A survey of these ACE women of color alumnae (Turner and Kappes, 2009) revealed numerous perceived benefits of the program, including networking opportunities and participating in workshops and seminars focused on specific skills (such as strategic planning). Despite the inclusion of women of color as program speakers, however, some participants in the Fellows program found that issues specific to race and equality were trivialized and that the program was "merely cloning the existing white male and female leadership styles that will produce the same result: few women of color at the helm" (Turner and Kappes, 2009, p. 165).

Responding to issues related to women of color specifically, the ACE Office of Women in Higher Education has sponsored two Women of Color summits (2006 and 2008) in addition to its national and regional leadership development and networking programs for women in general (American Council on Education, 2010). In addition, ACE recently launched the Spectrum Initiative, a national agenda with a key goal to "broaden and strengthen the leadership pipeline for women and racial/ethnic minority administrators and prepare them for senior leadership positions in higher education" (American Council on Education, 2010).

In addition to mentoring and formal training and development programs and institutes, other related strategies for promoting women in higher education leadership include learning from the advice of women who have attained these positions (see, for example, Bornstein, 2008; D. Cook, 2008; Moses, 2009), career mapping or intentional career planning (Moses, 2009; Santovec, 2007), promoting self-efficacy (Sloma-Williams, McDade, Richman, and Morahan, 2009), institutionalizing policies that enable women to manage both work and family (such as child-care facilities and flexible work schedules), increasing the number of women in the senior faculty pipeline and promoting them earlier, doing more to include women on search teams and as serious candidates (Bornstein, 2008), and involving an advocate with poststructural feminist perspectives for disrupting dominant discourses that support narrow and predominantly masculine views of what counts as credible leadership (Gordon, Iverson, and Allan, 2010).

Augmenting Infrastructures and Organizational Norms

Strategies for enhancing women's status and influence have also included approaches that advocate greater inclusion of women in formal administrative and leadership positions of the institution as well as the augmentation of existing institutional structures and practices. With a focus on reforming established institutional structures and related processes, these approaches are clearly conceptualized in a liberal feminist frame. Early examples include the establishment of Equal Employment Opportunity (EEO) and Affirmative Action Offices (catalyzed by policy) and more recently, the trend of assigning diversity and gender equity responsibilities to a high-level administrator like a vice president or vice provost—or ensuring that the EEO director reports directly to the institution's chief executive.

Generally speaking, a major responsibility of these offices and their administrators is to ensure compliance with institutional and public antidiscrimination policies. In addition, such offices can help to preserve institutional memory by serving as a repository of data gathered over the years—as opposed to such data's being dispersed throughout campus as task force and women's commission chairs come and go. Often these offices provide programmatic functions such as training and awareness related to campus climate. Further, a common function of the administrators serving in these programs is to follow up on discrimination complaints related to hiring, firing, salary, and identity-based harassment, including sexual harassment.

The establishment of campus women's centers is another approach to augmenting the extant institutional infrastructure. Largely focused on serving the needs of students, such centers date back to the 1960s women's movement and typically provide a physical space for women to assemble formally and informally. As well, they typically offer a venue for programmatic initiatives with an emphasis on women and women's contributions. Additionally, such centers may help organize formal and informal mentoring programs and professional development opportunities and serve as vehicles for grassroots organizing of professional staff and faculty women.

It could be argued that virtually all institutionalized programs to support gender equity or enforce antidiscrimination policies can be traced to influences of women's grassroots activism. An ongoing tension among feminists, however, is whether institutionalized programs can be as effective as grassroots initiatives or those positioned against the formal organizational hierarchy. Yet many feminists argue that positional power or formal authority (in the organization) is precisely what is needed to advance change. Numerous feminist women remain ambivalent, acknowledging the legitimacy of both perspectives and seeing their role and the role of women's centers and commissions as "within yet against" the institution (Allan, 2008).

The Women's Place at the Ohio State University is an example of an effort that became institutionalized in 2000 to coalesce initiatives of both formal and grassroots groups that had been working consistently for more than two decades to improve the climate for women (Ohio State University, 2010). The director of the office holds the title of associate provost, suggesting its place in the organizational hierarchy; the office's mission is to serve as "a catalyst for institutional change to expand opportunities for women's growth, leadership and power in an inclusive supportive and safe university environment" (Ohio State University, 2010). The work of the Women's Place includes leadership development programs, lectures focused on women or women's contributions, status-of-women reports, and a graduate women's network. Although many colleges and universities have offices, committees, task forces, or other programs that work toward similar goals, a great degree of variability is apparent in the stability, funding, and prestige of such initiatives.

Remedying gender-based salary inequities serves as another example of strategies that work to alter aspects of the formal infrastructure of postsecondary institutions. Although the Equal Pay Act of 1963 mandated equal pay for equal work, the wage gap persists, with women earning roughly 75 to 77 percent of what their male counterparts earn (Drago, 2010). In the context of postsecondary education, salaries are determined by a range of factors, including rank, educational attainment and qualifications, experience, and type of institution (that is, research-intensive institutions tend to pay higher salaries). Research specific to recently hired faculty confirms a wage gap for women faculty that is unexplained by other factors (Porter, Toutkoushian, and Moore, 2008). More specifically, female faculty members earn significantly less (4 to 6 percent) than their male counterparts in comparable ranks and institutions.

Recommendations to remedy gender-based salary inequity have evolved over time in light of research findings and in response to legal challenges and outcomes of litigation over gender-based pay inequity and pay discrimination. When gender-based pay inequities are found, salary adjustments can be made both across the board and individually (Eckes and Toutkoushian, 2006). Other strategies for salary inequity focus on prevention by examining pay differentials at time of hiring. Approaches that view gender bias as the root problem yield strategies that focus on training administrators to be more aware of potential biases that may contribute to overvaluing qualifications of male candidates. Other approaches contend that salaries would be more equitable at the time of hiring if women were socialized to be better negotiators. Thus, some strategies reflective of liberal and psychological feminist lenses involve training sessions and tips designed to help women acquire negotiating skills needed to attain salaries comparable to their male counterparts at time of hiring.

A different perspective is offered by Metcalfe and Slaughter (2008), who suggest that shifting prestige systems (from expert-based power of the traditional academy to market-based power in the entrepreneurial academy) place women at a disadvantage in terms of prestige, valuation, and compensation. In their analysis they argue this shift, also known as "academic capitalism" (Slaughter and Leslie, 1997; Slaughter and Rhoades, 2004), "creates conditions within colleges and universities that allow men to recapture some of the historic privilege they derived from higher education" (Metcalfe and Slaughter, 2008, p. 81). Drawing from both socialist and third-wave feminist lenses, the researchers suggest women position themselves strategically in light of the predominant academic capitalist knowledge and learning regime. They recommend scholars acknowledge how interconnections between the marketplace academy and the neoliberal state shift "public subsidy from welfare functions to entrepreneurial activity; [exhibit] preference for commercial solutions to public problems; [empower] managers rather than workers and the individual over the collective" (p. 101). Thus, they caution, "If women choose the academic capitalist knowledge/learning regime, they are in effect choosing the neoliberal state and closing down the network of public policies and agencies that made possible women's entry into the academy" (p. 101).

Numerous other approaches and strategies exist that tend to prioritize shifting attitudes and cultural norms rather than assuming that increased representation of women will lead to substantive change. In general the strategies in this group seek to alter attitudinal and behavioral barriers found to impede women's advancement and full participation in higher education and include those designed to (1) acknowledge the importance of, and provide support for, the emotional and household labor for which women continue to hold a greater share than their male counterparts; (2) build awareness of gender and race schemas serving as filters through which participants in higher education unconsciously reinscribe discriminatory practices (Valian, 1999; Sagaria, 2002); (3) challenge differential rewards for teaching and research; (4) build norms that place greater value on the "feminine" work of advising, community building, mentoring, and building webs of inclusion; (5) promote safe and welcoming environments for work and learning through enforcement of harassment and sexual harassment policies and strategies to prevent violations; and (6) promote more egalitarian communications and decision-making processes.

Curriculum Transformation, Pedagogy, and Knowledge Production

Creating more inclusive curricula and classrooms such as women's studies and women in the curriculum programs is another predominant strategy for promoting the status of women in higher education. Further, emerging from or connected to these initiatives are efforts to transform knowledge production through the development of feminist epistemology and centers for research on women. These curricular and research efforts are transformation oriented. Nevertheless, because they are housed in or maintain connections to institutions described as inherently patriarchal, the picture is more complex. Although they operate within, however, they are also working to disrupt and transform dominant masculine institutional structures and ways of knowing. This situation is in contrast to other strategies where the emphasis is more aptly described as "reform oriented" such as strategies to increase the number of women in the pipeline.

Schonberger's overview (2002) of historical and recent developments in women's studies and women in the curriculum efforts and Ropers-Huilman's overview (2002) of feminism in the academy provide important contextual perspectives and key themes relative to these change-oriented initiatives. The presence of women's studies, scholarship by and about women, and curriculum transformation efforts in colleges and universities has grown vastly since the late 1960s, when the first academic program was established at San Diego State University (Purcell, 2002). Today according to data gathered by the National Women's Studies Association (2010), at least 652 women's and gender studies programs are available at U.S. postsecondary institutions, and more than 85 percent of courses offered by these programs fulfill general education requirements. In addition, more than 30 percent of women's studies faculty are of color, compared with 19 percent of faculty nationally.

The growth of women's studies programs was paralleled and fueled by growth in research by and about women. Much of this research was catalyzed by the recognition that the established knowledge base of disciplines was male centered and failed to acknowledge women's contributions. Feminist scholars challenged and rejected the value-neutral and objective claims of positivist science and worked to produce an "awareness of the complexity, historical contingency, and fragility, of the practices we invent to discover truth" (Lather, 1990, p. 80). One outcome of these critiques and challenges has been the development of epistemologies and methodologies (Cook and Fonow, 1990; Harding, 1987; Lather, 1991) that seek to decenter privileged perspectives (white, male, heterosexual) inherent in predominant approaches to practicing science and propose methods of knowledge production aligned with feminist principles.

Feminist influences in epistemology and methodology are mirrored in pedagogy as well as with the development of practices designed to "foster equal access, participation, and engagement for all students in the learning process" (Maher and Tetreault, 2002, p. 130). Feminist pedagogy is always evolving but in general has worked to develop teaching strategies that create more student-centered classrooms through collaborative learning; evocation of student reactions and reflections in journals; shared classroom decision making; acknowledgment of differences in race, sexual identity, and social class; and student-led discussions, to name a few (Maher and Tetreault, 2002).

Efforts to expand traditional curricula to be more inclusive of women of color and their contributions reflect multicultural, global, and postcolonial feminist lenses. Scholarship by and about women of color and research that employs methodological approaches that foreground race, culture, and citizenship as important aspects of women's experiences are also examples of strategies emerging from these frames. *Sage: A Scholarly Journal of Black Women*, Collins's *Black Feminist Thought* (1991), and Walker's introduction of the word "womanism" (1983) as an alternative to black feminism are examples of such strategies from a multicultural perspective. The scholarly journal *Meridians: Feminism, Race, and Transnationalism;* Mohanty, Russo, and Torres's edited volume, *Third World Women and the Politics of Feminism* (1991), and Narayan's *Decentering the Center: Philosophy for a Multicultural, Postcolonial, and Feminist world* (2000) are examples of scholarship that applies a postcolonial feminist lens.

Summary

Strategies to enhance the status of women in higher education are numerous. This overview provided a snapshot of the range of approaches and change strategies commonly implemented to enhance gender equity in colleges and universities. With feminist activism as catalyst over time and across types of institutions, these strategies generally fall into one or more categories: policy and policy-related initiatives, mentoring, leadership development, altering institutional infrastructures and organizational norms, and curriculum transformation, feminist pedagogy, and knowledge production. Clearly, several feminist frames are more evident than others in key change strategies described in the literature. The following chapter takes a closer look at which frames are most prominent and considers potential implications for scholarship related to women's status in higher education.

Implications and Recommendations

EARLIER CHAPTERS DESCRIBING THE HISTORICAL CON-
TEXT and status of women in higher education document a number of
impressive gains for women in U.S. higher education since the 1960s. Yet
despite progress and concerted efforts to enhance women's status, inequities
persist. Scholars and policymakers point out that enhancing the representation of women across types of institutions and levels of academe will help create more inclusive and hospitable climates for men as well as women
(Touchton, Musil, and Campbell, 2008). Yet the intractability of inequity calls
for further research and more effective approaches to change.

What can be learned from the review provided in this monograph? First,
as delineated in Chapter One, it is important to place current trends in a historical context that considers "progress" for women in higher education against
the backdrop of an evolving sociopolitical landscape. In this light, impressive
gains are evident in terms of women's presence in higher education. Despite
these gains however, persistent inequities linked to gendered patterns of representation have been the subject of investigation by scholars who point to
long-term economic implications for women.

Recommendations for Further Research

In terms of access and representation of women in higher education, further
research is needed to better understand and remedy inequities that reflect intersections of identity differences among women, including race, sexual identity,

disability, and age. In particular the disparity in the representation of women of color calls for more scholarly attention and strategy development. Because "the higher the fewer" continues to characterize the uneven representation of women in the upper ranks of prestige hierarchies, more research is needed to better understand how to disrupt gendered patterns and norms that shape perceptions of prestige in and between institutions. Similarly, more studies are needed to enhance understandings of how to promote parity for women in leadership roles (including student leadership) and athletics. Such research will contribute to understanding factors and dynamics that both impede and accelerate the pace of change along the path to truly equitable representation for women students, staff, faculty, and administrators in higher education. Echoing conclusions drawn by numerous scholars, this monograph underscores the need to challenge overly simplistic claims that women's equitable representation has been attained and that gender equity initiatives are no longer relevant or necessary.

The research in the area of campus climate underscores complexities inherent in assessing equity. In sum, we know that gauging progress toward equity by numbers alone is insufficient. Although the representation of women is an important indicator, equity is far more nuanced than proportions can convey. Because climate often reflects the larger sociopolitical context, including underlying values and norms of the broader culture, and because colleges and universities are microcosms of the larger society, some climate-related themes are common for women in multiple roles on campus, regardless of whether they are students, professional staff, or senior leaders. Scholars contend the manner in which colleges and universities are organized, the way they conduct business, and what counts as legitimate knowledge tend to privilege masculinity and masculine approaches and thereby disadvantage women and men who are committed to more collaborative and generative approaches. Numerous factors contributing to inequitable climates have been identified, but more research is needed to better understand promising approaches to transforming aspects of campus climate found to disadvantage women while also identifying factors that help women to thrive alongside their male counterparts as students, faculty, staff, and administrators.

Implications

A range of theoretical frames in feminism offer diverse approaches to conceptualizing power, understanding complexities of inequity, and advancing strategies for change. Although this monograph highlights key characteristics that differentiate feminist schools of thought, it also emphasizes their common threads. Feminist theory is dynamic and evolving as interdisciplinary scholars continue to move it forward by extending previous work and blurring boundaries between schools of thought. More than a singular perspective, feminist theory offers a set of lenses refined over decades for the purpose of analyzing oppression and the promotion of equity in a range of contexts, including higher education.

Some feminist lenses are more evident than others in extant scholarship about gender equity in higher education. Although the overreliance on particular feminist lenses has been noted by other scholars (for example, Glazer-Raymo, 1999), little in-depth examination has occurred of the diversity of these lenses and potential implications for understanding, analyzing, and advancing women's status in higher education. A recent exception is Ropers-Huilman and Winters's (forthcoming) *Feminist Research in Higher Education*. Aligning with a key thesis of this monograph, the authors find it "troubling that multiple perspectives and frameworks offered by feminist scholars have not often been taken up within mainstream higher education outlets" (p. 25).

More specifically, the review of change strategies provided in the previous chapter suggests a strong reliance on liberal feminist perspectives. The myriad of strategies designed to promote equality of opportunities through enhancing recruitment; increasing availability of team sports; implementing and enforcing antidiscrimination policies; grooming, mentoring, and undertaking professional development to widen the pool of qualified applicants; and remedying salary disparities all reflect liberal feminist conceptualizations of power as a resource with the goal of redistributing that power more evenly between men and women.

Radical feminist influences are also evident in change strategies in the context of higher education. Efforts to develop and sustain women's spaces, knowledge by and about women, and valuing women's experiences, including the establishment of women's student centers, women's colleges, and women's or feminist research and writing groups represent some of the prominent transformative and women-centered approaches. Care-focused approaches informed by perspectives in a psychological feminist frame are reflected in change strategies that advocate for collective decision making and generative approaches to leadership that foreground the importance of networks, community, and empowerment.

The growing influence of multicultural, global, and postcolonial feminisms is reflected in the expansion of strategies that acknowledge identity differences among women. The particular strategies may be similar to those characterizing a range of feminist frames; however, they are distinguished by their acknowledgment of how racism and practices of colonization have shaped women's lives. For instance, Stromquist employs postcolonial and global feminist lenses in her *Feminist Organizations and Social Transformation in Latin America* (2006). Similarly, in *Knowledge Capital and Excellence: Implications of a Science-Centered University for Gender Equity* (2010), she examines the discursive shaping of ideas about higher education conveyed in policy documents put forth by the World Bank and the Inter-American Development Bank. Sue Rosser, who has contributed significantly to scholarship about women in STEM fields, describes how postcolonial feminism and international experiences in Kenya, Saskatchewan, and Sweden helped provide her with insights for understanding biases in the production of scientific knowledge: "The conscious de-development of southern continents under colonization by countries in northern continents in the nineteenth and early twentieth centuries created a historical backdrop in which centuries of indigenous knowledge of the environment, health, natural resources, and appropriate technologies were erased creating an atmosphere that allows most Western scientists to fail to challenge the notion that they have everything to give and nothing to learn from developing countries" (Rosser, 1999, p. 3). More recently Asher (2010) drew on postcolonial feminist perspectives to examine and interrogate the concept of academic leadership in the context of higher education.

In addition to scholarship and pedagogy informed by multicultural, global, and postcolonial feminism, policy and programmatic efforts have been developed from these perspectives. The Women of Color Summits sponsored by the American Council on Education and the Women of Color caucus of the National Women's Studies Association are two examples of initiatives at the national level and awards programs designed specifically to honor and acknowledge contributions made by women of color (for example, the 2010 Outstanding Women of Color in Education Awards).

In comparison, strategies for advancing women's status that explicitly reflect feminist Marxist or socialist, poststructural, and ecofeminist perspectives are less evident in the literature. At present these frames appear to be most often reflected in efforts to create space and support for new and different ways of knowing (and being) and the nurturing of alternative programs and institutions that align with values and conceptualizations of power characterizing these frames. In the sense that institutions of higher education employ feminist scholars who are producing scholarship from these perspectives, the academy can be understood as a vehicle for feminist scholars to challenge ways of knowing perceived to reinforce patriarchal, racist, colonial, and other systems considered to impede the attainment of equity for women.

Overreliance on liberal feminist approaches (arguably the most mainstream), however, may eclipse the availability and potential utility of strategies emerging from other feminist perspectives like ecofeminism and feminist poststructuralism. In light of stagnation in a number of areas and some signs of regression related to women's status in higher education (Glazer-Raymo, 2008a), the importance of new approaches cannot be underestimated. Perhaps the pace of change toward parity could be accelerated if more perspectives were drawn on to diagnose factors contributing to inequity and to develop solutions to remedy them.

In addition to the potential benefits of applying multiple frames, scholars have also pointed to the costs of not doing so. For instance, failure to draw on multiple perspectives for strategy development may unintentionally reinscribe *in*equity (Allan, 2008; Bensimon, 1995; De Castell and Bryson, 1997). For example, without a multicultural or global lens, problems related to the status of women in higher education are likely to be conceptualized in ways that foreground perspectives of white and Western women without accounting for how race and ethnicity shape experiences of inequity and difference among women; similarly, without a radical lens, heterosexism may not be recognized and particular challenges for lesbian women overlooked. Without an ecofeminist perspective, gender equity strategies may fail to fully dismantle logics of domination; without a feminist poststructural perspective, well-intended policymaking efforts may reinscribe inequity by drawing on dominant discourses that tend to result in the framing of gender equity as a problem of women's deficiency (for example, lack of sufficient mentoring, lack of professional credentials, or lack of confidence) rather than a problem of institutional structures and practices that privilege particular perspectives and identities.

Recommendations for Practice

Praxis, the integration of theory and practice, is a core principle of feminist scholarship (Lather, 1991; Bracken, Allen, and Dean, 2006). Familiarity with a range of feminist theories can help broaden perspectives on power and root causes of gender inequity. In so doing these lenses can serve scholars and practitioners by enhancing understandings of complexities and nuances shaping women's lives and their status in higher education. The diversity of perspectives can also help expand the repertoire of change strategies available to inform research but also *action* based on that research. In the spirit of praxis and considering practical ways to build on insights provided by this review, three key recommendations emerge:

Promote and support opportunities to learn about women's experiences in general and in higher education. Although feminist theories are not the only way to think about enhancing women's status, they represent a particularly rich and interdisciplinary body of scholarship related to the goal of building more egalitarian and socially just communities. Those supporting and engaged in efforts to enhance women's status in higher education can begin by sharpening their knowledge of the diversity of feminist perspectives. Sharing the second chapter of this monograph or a similar synopsis of feminist frames and drawing on campus resources such as faculty and graduate students who have studied feminist theory may be helpful for administrators, committee members, and participants in ad hoc working groups focused on gender equity.

Analyze gender equity problems and solutions through multiple feminist frames. Being familiar with a range of theoretical frames is an important beginning, but knowledge does not always translate to action. Putting feminist frames to use is a vital next step. Thinking both broadly and within one's sphere of influence, this recommendation urges readers to examine particular gender equity challenges through multiple lenses. In practical terms, it involves developing deliberate strategies to make assumptions about root causes of the problem and inherent power dynamics explicit. For those seeking more structure to operationalize this recommendation, Exhibits 1 and 2 can serve as starting points.

Develop and implement change strategies (both inside and outside postsecondary institutions) that reflect a range of feminist perspectives. This monograph has documented gains, persistent problems, and continuing complexities related to enhancing women's status in higher education. It is clear no single approach or remedy exists, but some perspectives are more prominent than others in shaping understandings of and responses to identified problems. Although it may be argued the resulting strategies have been useful, evidence suggests they are insufficient and, moreover, tend to eclipse the availability of other potentially effective approaches. Thus although we may choose to support and implement feminist approaches that have proven useful, we should simultaneously work to expand the implementation of strategies that reflect a greater diversity of perspectives.

Summing Up

A primary purpose of this monograph was to review scholarly literature on the status of women in higher education and to analyze predominant approaches to advancing women's status. Although gaps remain, this review confirms that scholarship related to women's status in higher education is evolving and deepening in a number of ways. For example, we know more about the representation of women than we do about aspects of campus climate that contribute to women's status. We know that judging progress toward equity by aggregate numbers alone yields a warped image of equity attained. Yet the more we acknowledge and uncover the complexities, the more questions arise calling for continued exploration.

Further research and activism are essential for maintaining gains for women in higher education and to increase the pace of change needed to ensure all participants in higher education are afforded equitable treatment, opportunities, and climates in which to thrive and achieve their full potential. Understanding and applying multiple feminist lenses holds promise for extending what we know and for expanding possibilities of transformative change. This review of the literature confirms that equity still matters in higher education. For scholars and practitioners committed to promoting equity and advancing more inclusive and socially just educational environments, feminist theory can provide vitally important perspectives for framing the problems and advancing solutions.

References

Acosta, R. V., and Carpenter, L. J. (2010). *Women in intercollegiate sport: A longitudinal, national study, thirty-three year update.* http://www.acostacarpenter.org/2010pdf%20 combined%20final.pdf

Adair, V. C. (2002). Overview. In A. M. Martínez Alemán and K. A. Renn (Eds.), *Women in higher education: An encyclopedia* (pp. 205–211). Santa Barbara, CA: ABC-CLIO.

Adair, V. C., and Dahlberg, S. L. (Eds.). (2003). *Reclaiming class: Women, poverty, and the promise of higher education in America.* Philadelphia: Temple University Press.

Adelman, C. (2006). *The toolbox revisited: Paths to degree completion from high school through college.* Washington, DC: U.S. Department of Education.

Adelman, H. S., and Taylor, L. (2005). Classroom climate. In S. W. Lee, P. A. Lowe, and E. Robinson (Eds.), *Encyclopedia of school psychology.* Thousand Oaks, CA: Sage.

Aisenberg, N., and Harrington, M. (1988). *Women of academe: Outsiders in the sacred grove.* Amherst: University of Massachusetts Press.

Allan, E. J. (2003). Constructing women's status: Policy discourses of university women's commission reports. *Harvard Educational Review, 73*(1), 44–72.

Allan, E. J. (2008). *Policy discourses, gender, and education: Constructing women's status.* New York: Routledge.

Allan, E. J., Gordon, S. V., and Iverson, S. (2006). Re/thinking practices of power: The discursive framing of leadership in *The Chronicle of Higher Education. Review of Higher Education, 30*(1), 41–68.

Allan, E. J., Iverson, S., and Ropers-Huilman, R. (Eds.). (2010). *Reconstructing policy in higher education: Feminist poststructural perspectives.* New York: Routledge.

Allan, E. J., and Madden, M. (2006). Chilly classrooms for female undergraduate students: A question of method. *Journal of Higher Education, 77*(4), 684–711.

Allen, A. (1999). *The power of feminist theory: Domination, resistance, solidarity.* Boulder, CO: Westview Press.

Allen, A. (2005). Feminist perspectives on power. *Stanford encyclopedia of philosophy.* Retrieved May 20, 2010, from http://plato.stanford.edu/entries/feminist-power/.

Altman, M. (2007). Mentors and tormentors. *NWSA Journal, 19*(3), 182–189.

American Association of University Women. (2010). *Sexual assault on campus.* Retrieved January 1, 2011, from http://www.aauw.org/act/laf/library/assault.cfm.

American Association of University Women, Sexual Harassment Task Force. (2004). *Harassment-free hallways: How to stop sexual harassment in school.* Washington, DC: American Association of University Women Educational Foundation.

American Association of University Women Educational Foundation, Commission on Technology, Gender, and Teacher Education (2000). *Tech-savvy: Educating girls in the new computer age.* Washington, DC: American Association of University Women Educational Foundation.

American Council on Education. (2010). Spectrum initiative: Advancing diversity in the college presidency. Retrieved September 10, 2010, from http://www.acenet.edu/Content/NavigationMenu/ProgramsServices/CAREE/ProgramsInitiatives/Spectrum.htm.

American Council on Education, Office of Women in Higher Education. (2010). Web site. Retrieved September 10, 2010, from http://www.acenet.edu/AM/Template.cfm?Section=OWHE.

American Council on Education. (2005). *Forty college faculty and administrators named to ACE fellows program.* Retrieved September 15, 2010, from http://www.acenet.edu/AM/Template.cfm?Section=Home&TEMPLATE=/CM/ContentDisplay.cfm&CONTENTID=19977.

American Federation of Teachers Higher Education. (2009). *American academic: The state of the higher education workforce 1997–2007.* Washington, DC: American Federation of Teachers.

Amey, M. J., and Eddy, P. L. (2002). Leadership. In A. M. Martínez Alemán and K. A. Renn (Eds.), *Women in higher education* (pp. 482–486). Santa Barbara, CA: ABC-CLIO.

Amey, M. J., and Twombly, S. B. (1992). Re-visioning leadership in community colleges. *Review of Higher Education, 15*(2), 125–150.

Anderson, D. J., Cheslock, J. J., and Ehrenberg, R. G. (2006). Gender equity in intercollegiate athletics: Determinants of Title IX compliance. *Journal of Higher Education, 77*(2), 225–250.

Asher, N. (2010). How does the postcolonial, feminist academic lead? A perspective from the US south. *International Journal of Leadership in Education, 13*(1), 63–76.

Association of American Colleges and Universities. (2010). *Program on the status and education of women.* Retrieved September 10, 2010, from http://www.aacu.org/psew/index .cfm.

Association of Governing Boards of Universities and Colleges. (2010a). *Policies, practices, and composition of governing boards of public colleges, universities, and systems: Executive summary.* Washington, DC: Association of Governing Boards of Universities and Colleges.

Association of Governing Boards of Universities and Colleges. (2010b). *Policies, practices, and composition of governing boards of independent colleges and universities: Executive summary.* Washington, DC: Association of Governing Boards of Universities and Colleges.

Astin, A. W. (1977). *Four critical years: Effects of college on beliefs, attitudes, and knowledge.* San Francisco: Jossey-Bass.

Astin, A. W. (1993). *What matters in college? Four critical years revisited.* San Francisco: Jossey-Bass.

Astin, H. S. (1984). The meaning of work in women's lives: A sociopsychological model of career choice and work behavior. *Counseling Psychologist, 12*(4), 117–126.

Astin, H. S., and Leland, C. (1991). *Women of influence, women of vision: A cross-generational study of leaders and change.* San Francisco: Jossey-Bass.

August, L., and Waltman, J. (2004). Culture, climate, and contribution: Career satisfaction among female faculty. *Research in Higher Education, 45*, 177–192.

Bacchi, C. L. (1999). *Women, policy and politics: The construction of policy problems.* Thousand Oaks, CA: Sage.

Ball, S. J. (1990). *Politics and policy making in education: Explorations in policy sociology.* New York: Routledge.

Ball, S. J. (1994). *Education reform: A critical and post-structural approach.* Buckingham, UK: Open University Press.

Banks, T. (1988). Gender bias in the classroom. *Journal of Legal Education, 38*, 137–146.

Basow, S. (1995). Student evaluations of college professors: When gender matters. *Journal of Educational Psychology, 87*(4), 656–665.

Baxter, J. (2003). *Positioning gender in discourse: A feminist methodology.* New York: Palgrave Macmillan.

Becker, W. E., and Toutkoushian, R. K. (2003). Measuring gender bias in the salaries of tenured faculty members. *New Directions for Institutional Research* (No. 117, pp. 5–20). San Francisco: Jossey-Bass.

Belenky, M. F., Clinchy, B. M., Goldberger, N. R., and Tarule, J. M. (1986). *Women's ways of knowing: The development of self, voice and mind.* New York: Basic Books.

Bellas, M. L. (1993). Faculty salaries: Still a cost of being female? *Social Science Quarterly, 74*(1), 62–75.

Bensimon, E. M. (1991). The social processes through which faculty shape the image of a new president. *Journal of Higher Education, 62*(6), 637–660.

Bensimon, E. M. (1995). Total quality management in the academy: A rebellious reading. *Harvard Educational Review, 65*(4), 593–612.

Bensimon, E. M., and Marshall, C. (1997). Policy analysis for postsecondary education: Feminist and critical perspectives. In C. Marshall (Ed.), *Feminist critical policy analysis II: A perspective from post-secondary education* (pp. 1–21). Washington, DC: Falmer Press.

Bensimon, E. M., and Marshall, C. (2000). Policy analysis for postsecondary education: Feminist and critical perspectives. In J. Glazer-Raymo, B. K. Townsend, and R. Ropers-Huilman (Eds.), *Women in higher education: A feminist perspective* (2nd ed., pp. 133–147). Boston: Pearson Custom Publishing.

Bensimon, E. M., and Marshall, C. (2003). Like it or not: Feminist critical policy analysis matters. *Journal of Higher Education, 74*(3), 337–349.

Bensimon, E. M., Neumann, A., and Birnbaum, R. (1989). Higher education and leadership theory. Making sense of administrative leadership (ASHE-ERIC Research Report No. 1). Reprinted in M. C. Brown (Ed.), (2000), *Organization and governance in higher education* (5th ed., pp. 214–222). Boston: Pearson Custom Publishing.

Berry, T. R., and Mizelle, N. (Eds.). (2006). *From oppression to grace: Women of color and their dilemmas within the academy*. Sterling, VA: Stylus Publishing.

Blackmore, J. (1999). *Troubling women: Feminism, leadership, and educational change*. Philadelphia: Open University Press.

Blickenstaff, J. C. (2005). Women and science careers: Leaky pipeline or gender filter? *Gender and Education, 17*(4), 369–386.

Bok, D. (1990). *Universities and the future of America*. Durham, NC: Duke University Press.

Bornstein, R. (2008). Women and the college presidency. In J. Glazer-Raymo (Ed.), *Unfinished agendas: New and continuing gender challenges in higher education* (pp. 162–184). Baltimore: Johns Hopkins University Press.

Bowen, H. R., and Schuster, J. H. (1986). *American professors: A national resource imperiled*. Fair Lawn, NJ: Oxford University Press.

Bracken, S., Allen, J., and Dean, D. (2006). *The balancing act: Gendered perspectives in faculty roles and lives*. Sterling, VA: Stylus.

Brady, K. L., and Eisler, R. M. (1999). Sex and gender equity in the college classroom: A quantitative analysis of faculty-student interactions and perceptions. *Journal of Educational Psychology, 9*(1), 127–145.

Braidotti, R. (1994). *Nomadic subjects: Embodiment and sexual difference in contemporary feminist thought*. New York: Columbia University Press.

Brooks, V. R. (1982). Sex differences in student dominance behavior in female and male professors' classrooms. *Sex Roles, 8*, 683–690.

Brown, H. (2009, October 6). Women college presidents' tough test. *Forbes*. Retrieved November 15, 2010, from http://www.forbes.com.

Bunch, C. (1987). *Passionate politics: Feminist theory in action*. New York: St. Martin's.

Bunch, C., and Pollack, S. (Eds.). (1983). *Learning our way: Essays in feminist education*. Trumansburg, NY: The Crossing Press.

Campus Compact. (2003). *Service statistics: Highlights of Campus Compact's annual membership survey*. Retrieved September 12, 2010, from http://www.compact.org/newscc/ 2003_Statistics.pdf.

Carpenter, L. J., and Acosta, R. V. (2010). *Women in intercollegiate sport: A longitudinal, national study thirty-three year update*. West Brookfield, MA: Acosta/Carpenter.

Center for Public Integrity (2010). *Sexual assault on campus: A frustrating search for justice*. Retrieved September 15, 2010, from http://www.publicintegrity.org/investigations/ campus_assault/.

Chamberlain, M. K. (1988). *Women in academe: Progress and prospects*. New York: Russell Sage Foundation.

Chism, N. V. (1999). Taking student social diversity into account. In W. J. McKeachie (Ed.), *Teaching tips: Strategies, research, and theory for college and university teachers* (10th ed., pp. 218–233). Boston: Houghton Mifflin.

Chliwniak, L. (1997). *Higher education leadership: Analyzing the gender gap* (ASHE-ERIC Higher Education Report 25). Washington, DC: George Washington University.

Christ, C. P. (2003). *She who changes: Re-imagining the divine in the world*. New York: Palgrave Macmillan.

Collins, P. H. (1991). *Black feminist thought: Knowledge, consciousness, and the politics of empowerment.* New York: Routledge.

Constantinople, A., Cornelius, R., and Gray, J. (1988). The chilly climate: Fact or artifact? *Journal of Higher Education, 59,* 527–550.

Conway, M. M., Ahern, D. W., and Steuernagel, G. A. (1999). *Women and public policy: A revolution in progress* (2nd ed.). Washington, DC: CQ Press.

Cook, B. J., and Cordova, D. I. (2007). *Minorities in higher education: Twenty-second annual status report, 2007 supplement.* Washington, DC: American Council on Education.

Cook, D. (2008). Some historical perspectives on professionalism. In B. Cunningham (Ed.), *Exploring professionalism* (pp. 10–27). London, UK: Bedford Wall Papers.

Cook, J. A., and Fonow, M. M. (1990). Knowledge and women's interests: Issues of epistemology and methodology in feminist sociological research. In J. M. Nielsen (Ed.), *Feminist research methods: Exemplary readings in the social sciences* (pp. 69–93). Boulder, CO: Westview Press.

Cook, S. G. (2008). Radcliffe alumnae prod Harvard toward gender equity. *Women in Higher Education, 17*(9), 1–2.

Cooper, J., and others. (2007). Improving gender equity in postsecondary education. In S. S. Klein, B. Richardson, D. A. Grayson, L. H. Fox, C. Kramarae, D. S. Pollard, and C. A. Dwyer (Eds.), *Handbook for achieving gender equity through education* (2nd ed., pp. 631–653). Mahwah, NJ: Lawrence Erlbaum Associates.

Cooper, J. E., and Stevens, D. D. (2002). The journey toward tenure. In J. E. Cooper and D. D. Stevens (Eds.), *Tenure in the sacred grove: Issues and strategies for women and minority faculty* (pp. 3–15). Albany: State University of New York Press.

Corbett, C., Hill, C., and St. Rose, A. (2008). *Where the girls are: The facts about gender equity in education.* Washington, DC: AAUW Educational Foundation.

Cornelius, R. R., Gray, J. M., and Constantinople, A. P. (1990). Student-faculty interaction in the college classroom. *Journal of Research and Development in Education, 23,* 189–197.

Coser, L. A. (1974). *Greedy institutions: Patterns of undivided commitment.* New York: Free Press.

Crawford, M., and MacLeod, M. (1990). Gender in the college classroom: An assessment of the "chilly climate" for women. *Sex Roles, 23*(3/4), 101–122.

Crenshaw, K. (1997). Intersectionality and identity politics: Learning from violence against women of color. In M. L. Shanley and U. Narayan (Eds.), *Reconstructing political theory: Feminist perspectives* (pp. 178–193). University Park: Pennsylvania State University Press.

Cress, C. (2002). Campus climate. In A. M. Martínez Alemán and K. A. Renn (Eds.), *Women in higher education: An encyclopedia* (pp. 390–397). Santa Barbara, CA: ABC-CLIO.

Daly, M. (1978). *Gyn/ecology: The metaethics of radical feminism.* Boston: Beacon Press.

Daly, M. (1984). *Pure lust: Elemental feminist philosophy.* Boston: Beacon Press.

Davis, F. (1999). *Moving the mountain: The women's movement in America since 1960.* New York: Simon & Schuster.

Dean, D. R. (2009). Resources, role models, and opportunity makers: Mentoring women in academic leadership. In D. R., Dean, S. J., Bracken, and J. K., Allen (Eds.), *Women in academic leadership: Professional strategies, personal choices* (pp. 128–148) Sterling, VA: Stylus.

Dean, D. R., Bracken, S. J., and Allen, J. K. (Eds.) (2009). *Women in academic leadership: Professional strategies, personal choices*. Sterling, VA: Stylus.

De Castell, S., and Bryson, M. (Eds.). (1997). *Radical in(ter)ventions: Identity, politics, and difference/s in educational praxis*. Albany: State University of New York Press.

Dinnerstein, D. (1989). What does feminism mean? In A. Harris and Y. King (Eds.), *Rocking the ship of state: Toward a feminist peace politics*. Boulder, CO: Westview Press.

Dominici, F., Fried, L. P., and Zeger, S. L. (2009). So few women leaders. *Academe, 95*(4), 25–27.

Donovan, J. (1993). *Feminist theory: The intellectual traditions of American feminism*. New York: Continuum Publishing Company.

Drago, R. (2010). The gender wage gap 2009 (updated September 2010). Institute for Women's Policy Research, IWPR #C350.

Drew, T. L., and Work, G. G. (1998). Gender-based differences in perception of experiences in higher education: Gaining a broader perspective. *Journal of Higher Education, 69*, 542–555.

Eckes, S. E., and Toutkoushian, R. K. (2006). Legal issues and statistical approaches to reverse pay discrimination in higher education. *Research in Higher Education, 47*(8), 957–984.

Eddy, P. L. (2002). Presidency. In A. M. Martínez Alemán and K. A. Renn (Eds.), *Women in higher education* (pp. 498–502). Santa Barbara, CA: ABC-CLIO.

Eddy, P. L., and Cox, E. M. (2008). Gendered leadership: An organizational perspective. *New Directions for Community Colleges* (No. 142, pp. 69–79).

Eddy, P. L., and VanDerLinden, K. E. (2006). Emerging definitions of leadership in higher education: New visions of leadership or the same old "hero" leader? *Community College Review, 34*(1), 5–26.

Eisenstein, Z. (Ed.). (1979). *Capitalist patriarchy and the case for socialist feminism*. New York: Monthly Review Press.

Enloe, C. (1990). *Bananas, beaches, and bases: Making feminist sense of international politics*. Berkeley: University of California Press.

Estler, S. E., and Nelson, L. J. (2005). Who calls the shots? Sports and university leadership, culture, and decision making. *ASHE Higher Education Report, 30*(5). San Francisco: Jossey-Bass.

Evers, F., Livernois, J., and Mancuso, M. (2006). Where are the boys? Gender imbalance in higher education. *Higher Education Management and Policy, 18*(2), 1–25.

Ferree, M. M., and McQuillan, J. (1998). Gender-based pay gaps: Methodological and policy issues in university salary studies. *Gender & Society, 12*(1), 7–39.

Festle, M. J. (1996). *Playing nice: Politics and apologies in women's sports*. New York: Columbia University Press.

Fine, M. (1988). Sexuality, schooling and adolescent females: The missing discourse of desire. *Harvard Educational Review, 58*(1), 25.

Firestone, S. (1970). *The dialectic of sex.* New York: Bantam Books.

Fisher, B. S., Cullen, F. T., and Turner, M. T. (2000). *The sexual victimization of college women.* Research report 182369. Washington, DC: National Institute of Justice, U.S. Department of Justice.

Follet, C. V., Andberg, W. L., and Hendel, D. D. (1982). Perceptions of the college environment by women and men students. *Journal of College Student Personnel, 23,* 525–531.

Ford, J. (2006). Discourses of leadership. *Leadership, 2*(1), 77–99.

Foster, T. J., and Foster, M. S. (1994). *An empirical test of Hall and Sandler's 1982 report: Who finds the classroom chilly?* Paper presented at the Central States Communication Association Convention, April, Oklahoma City, OK.

Foucault, M. (1978). *The history of sexuality: An introduction* (Vol. 1). New York, NY: Random House.

Foucault, M. (1979). *Discipline & Punishment: The birth of the prison.* New York, NY: Random House.

Frankenberg, R. (1993). *White women, race matters: The social construction of whiteness.* London, UK: Routledge.

Fraser, N. (1989). *Unruly practices: Power, discourse, and gender in contemporary social theory.* Minneapolis: University of Minnesota Press.

Fraser, N., and Gordon, L. (1994). A genealogy of dependency: Tracing a keyword of the U.S. welfare state. *Signs: Journal of Women in Culture and Society, 19*(2), 309–336.

Freeman, J. (1973). Women on the move: Roots of revolt. In A. S. Rossi and A. Calderwood (Eds.), *Academic women on the move* (pp. 1–32). New York: Russell Sage Foundation.

French, M. (1985). *Beyond power: On women, men, and morals.* New York: Summit Books.

Gilligan, C. (1982). *In a different voice.* Cambridge, MA: Harvard University Press.

Gilmartin, S. K., and Sax, L. J. (2002). Romantic relationships. In A. M. Martínez Alemán and K. A. Renn (Eds.), *Women in higher education: An encyclopedia* (pp. 343–347). Santa Barbara, CA: ABC-CLIO.

Glazer-Raymo, J. (1999). *Shattering the myths: Women in academe.* Baltimore: Johns Hopkins University Press.

Glazer-Raymo, J. (2007). Gender equality in the American research university: Renewing the agenda for women's rights. In M. D. Sagaria (Ed.), *Women, universities and change: Gender equality in the European Union and the United States* (pp. 161–178). New York: Palgrave Macmillan.

Glazer-Raymo, J. (2008a). The feminist agenda: A work in progress. In J. Glazer-Raymo (Ed.), *Unfinished agendas: New and continuing gender challenges in higher education* (pp. 1–34). Baltimore: Johns Hopkins University Press.

Glazer-Raymo, J. (Ed.). (2008b). *Unfinished agendas: New and continuing gender challenges in higher education.* Baltimore: John Hopkins University Press.

Glazer-Raymo, J. (2008c). Women on governing boards: Why gender matters. In J. Glazer-Raymo (Ed.), *Unfinished agendas: New and continuing gender challenges in higher education* (pp. 185–210). Baltimore: Johns Hopkins University Press.

Glazer-Raymo, J., Townsend, B. K., and Ropers-Huilman, R. (Eds.). (2000). *Women in higher education: A feminist perspective* (2nd ed.). Boston: Pearson Custom Publishing.

Gordon, S., Iverson, S. V., and Allan, E. J. (2010). The discursive framing of women leaders in higher education. In E. J. Allan, S. V. Iverson, and R. Ropers-Huilman (Eds.), *Reconstructing policy in higher education: Feminist poststructural perspectives* (pp. 81–105). New York: Routledge.

Goulden, M., Frasch, K., and Mason, M. A. (2009). *Staying competitive: Patching America's leaky pipeline in the sciences*. Washington, DC: Center for American Progress.

Grady, M. L. (2002). American Indian administrators. In A. M. Martínez Alemán and K. A. Renn (Eds.), *Women in higher education: An encyclopedia* (pp. 469–472). Santa Barbara, CA: ABC-CLIO.

Grant, L., Kennelly, I., and Ward, K. B. (2000). Revisiting the gender, marriage, and parenthood puzzle in scientific careers. *Women's Studies Quarterly, 28*(1/2), 62–85.

Grappendorf, H., Pent, A., Burton, L., and Henderson, A. (2008). Gender role stereotyping: A qualitative analysis of senior woman administrators' perceptions regarding financial decision making. *Journal of Issues in Intercollegiate Athletics, 1*, 26–45.

Griffin, P. (1998). *Strong women, deep closets: Lesbians and homophobia in sport*. Champaign, IL: Human Kinetics Publishers.

Griffin, S. (1978). *Woman and nature: The roaring inside her*. New York: Harper & Row.

Hagedorn, L. S. (Ed.). (2000). Conceptualizing faculty job satisfaction: Components, theories, and outcomes. *New Directions for Institutional Research* (No. 105, pp. 5–20). San Francisco: Jossey-Bass.

Hall, R. M., and Sandler, B. R. (1982). *The classroom climate: A chilly one for women?* Washington, DC: Project on the Status and Education of Women, Association of American Colleges.

Harding, S. (1987). Introduction: Is there a feminist method? In S. E. Harding (Ed.), *Feminism and methodology* (pp. 1–14). Bloomington: Indiana University.

Harding, S. (1991). *Whose science? Whose knowledge? Thinking from women's lives*. Ithaca, NY: Cornell University.

Harding, S. (1993). *The "racial" economy of science: Toward a democratic future*. Bloomington: Indiana University Press.

Hargens, L. L., and Long, J. S. (2002). Demographic inertia and women's representation among faculty in higher education. *Journal of Higher Education, 73*(4), 494–517.

Hart, J. (2006). Women and feminism in higher education scholarship. *Journal of Higher Education, 77*(1), 40–61.

Hart, J., and Cress, C. (2008). Are women faculty just worrywarts? Accounting for gender differences in self-reported stress. *Journal of Human Behavior in the Social Environment, 17*(1–2), 175–193.

Hart, J., and Fellabaum, J. (2008). Analyzing campus climate studies: Seeking to define and understand. *Journal of Diversity in Higher Education, 1*(4), 222–234.

Hart, J., and Hubbard, J. (2010). Consuming higher education: Who is paying the price? In E. J. Allan, S. V. Iverson, and R. Ropers-Huilman (Eds.), *Reconstructing policy in higher education: Feminist poststructural perspectives* (pp. 147–165). New York: Routledge.

Hartmann, H. I. (1981). The unhappy marriage of Marxism and feminism: Towards a more progressive union. In L. Sargent (Ed.), *Women and revolution: A discussion of the unhappy marriage of Marxism and feminism* (pp. 1–41). Cambridge, MA: South End Press.

Hawkesworth, M. E. (1988). *Theoretical issues in policy analysis.* Albany: State University of New York Press.

Hawkesworth, M. E. (1994). Policy studies within a feminist frame. *Policy Sciences, 27,* 97–118.

Helgesen, S. (1990). *The female advantage: Women's ways of leadership.* New York: Currency/Doubleday.

Helgesen, S. (1995). *The web of inclusion.* New York: Currency/Doubleday.

Hennessy, R. (1993). *Materialist feminism and the politics of difference.* New York: Routledge.

Hennessy, R., and Ingraham, C. (1997). *Materialist feminism: A reader in class, difference, and women's lives.* London, UK: Routledge.

Hill, C., and Silva, E. (2005). *Drawing the line: Sexual harassment on campus.* Washington, DC: American Association of University Women Educational Foundation.

Hochschild, A. R. (1997). *The time bind: When work becomes home and home becomes work.* New York: Metropolitan Books.

Hoffer, T. B., and others. (2007). *Doctorate recipients from United States universities: Summary report 2006.* Chicago: National Opinion Research Center. Retrieved December 1, 2010, from http://www.norc.org/NR/rdonlyres/ 2E87F80C-82F6-4E26-9F78-CA4C6E0B79C6/0/sed2005.pdf.

Hoffman, J. L. (forthcoming). The old boys network: Women candidates and the athletic director search among NCAA division I programs. *Journal of Study of Sports and Athletes in Education.*

Hoffman, J. L., Iverson, S. V., Allan, E. J., and Ropers-Huilman, R. (2010). Title IX policy and intercollegiate athletics: A feminist poststructural critique. In E. J. Allan, S. V. Iverson, and R. Ropers-Huilman (Eds.), *Reconstructing policy in higher education: Feminist poststructural perspectives* (pp. 129–146). New York: Routledge.

Holland, D., and Eisenhart, M. (1992). *Educated in romance: Women, achievement and college culture.* Chicago: University of Chicago Press.

Hooks, B. (1984). *Feminist theory from margin to center.* Boston: South End Press.

Hurtado, S., Carter, D. F., and Kardia, D. (1998). The climate for diversity: Key issues for institutional self-study. In K. Bauer (Ed.), *Campus climate: Understanding the critical components of today's colleges and universities* (pp. 53–63). San Francisco: Jossey-Bass.

Hurtado, S., Clayton-Pedersen, A. R., Allen, W. R., and Milem, J. F. (1998). Enhancing campus climates for racial/ethnic diversity: Educational policy and practice. *Review of Higher Education, 21*(3), 279–302.

Hurtado, S., Milem, J., Clayton-Pedersen, A., and Walter, A. (1999). *Enacting diverse learning environments: Improving the climate for racial/ethnic diversity in higher education.* ASHE-ERIC Higher Education Report (Vol. 26, No. 8). Washington, DC: Graduate School of Education and Human Development, George Washington University.

Hussar, W. J., and Bailey, T. M. (2009). *Projections of education statistics to 2018* (NCES Report No. 2009-062). Washington, DC: National Center for Education Statistics, Institute of Education Sciences. U.S. Department of Education.

Institute of International Education. (2010). Open doors data: U.S. study abroad student Profile 1999/00–2008/09. Retrieved June 1, 2010, from http://www.iie.org/en/Research-and-Publications/Open-Doors/Data/US-Study-Abroad/Student-Profile/1999–2009.

Iverson, S. V. (2005). *A policy discourse analysis of U.S. land-grant university diversity action plans.* Unpublished doctoral dissertation, University of Maine, Orono, ME.

Iverson, S. V. (2007). Camouflaging power and privilege: A critical race analysis of university diversity policies. *Educational Administration Quarterly, 43*(5), 586–611.

Iverson, S. V. (2009). Crossing boundaries: Understanding women's advancement from clerical to professional positions. *NASPA Journal About Women in Higher Education, 2*(1), 140–166.

Jablonski, M. (1996). The leadership challenge for women college presidents. *Initiatives, 57*(4), 1–10.

Jaggar, A. M. (1983). *Feminist politics and human nature.* Oxford, UK: Rowman & Littlefield.

Jaschik, S. (2009, January 15). Rejecting the academic fast track. *Inside Higher Ed.* Retrieved May 1, 2010, from http://www.insidehighered.com/news/2009/01/15/family.

Jaschik, S. (2006). Affirmative action for men. *Inside Higher Ed.* Retrieved May 1, 2010, from http://www.insidehighered.com/news/.

Johnsrud, L. K. (2002). Measuring the quality of faculty and administrative worklife: Implications for college and university campuses. *Research in Higher Education, 43*(3), 379–395.

Johnsrud, L. K., and Rosser, V. J. (2002). Faculty members' morale and their intention to leave: A multilevel explanation. *Journal of Higher Education, 73*(4), 518–542.

June, A. W. (2009, April 20). Family-friendly policies may not help as much as they should, conference speaker says. *Chronicle of Higher Education.* Retrieved May 1, 2010, from http://chronicle.com.

Kezar, A. (2002). Expanding notions of leadership to capture pluralistic voices: Positionality theory in practice. *Journal of College Student Development, 43*(4), 558–578.

Kezar, A., Carducci, R., and Contreras-McGavin, M. (2006). *Rethinking the "L" word in higher education.* San Francisco: Jossey-Bass.

Kezar, A., and Moriarty, D. (2000). Expanding our understanding of student leadership development: A study exploring gender and ethnic identity. *Journal of College Student Development, 41*(1), 55–69.

King, J. E. (2000). *Gender equity in higher education: Are male students at a disadvantage?* Washington, DC: American Council on Education.

King, J. E. (2006). *Gender equity in higher education: 2006.* Washington DC: American Council on Education.

King, J. E. (2010). *Gender equity in higher education: 2010.* Washington, DC: American Council on Education, Center for Policy Analysis.

King, J. E., and Gomez, G. G. (2008). *On the pathway to the presidency: Characteristics of higher education's senior leadership.* Washington, DC: American Council on Education.

King, Y. (1989). The ecology of feminism and the feminism of ecology. In J. Plant (Ed.), *Healing the wounds: The promise of ecofeminism* (pp. 201–211). Philadelphia, PA: New Society.

Kingsbury, A. (2007, June 25). Admittedly unequal. *U.S. News & World Report,* pp. 50–53.

Kinzie, J., and others. (n.d.). *The relationship between gender and student engagement in college.* Unpublished manuscript.

Klein, S. S., and others. (Eds.). (2007). Handbook for achieving gender equity through eduation (2nd ed.). Mahwah, NJ: Lawrence Erlbaum Associates.

Knapp, L., Kelly-Reid, J. E., Whitmore, R. W., and Miller, E. (2007). Employees in postsecondary institutions, Fall 2005. Retrieved March 11, 2011, from http://nces.ed.gov/pubsearch/pubsinfo.asp?pubid=2007150.

Kolmar, W. K., and Bartkowski, F. (2010). *Feminist theory.* Boston: McGraw-Hill.

Koss, M. P., Gidycz, C. A., and Wisniewski, N. (1987). The scope of rape: Incidence and prevalence of sexual aggression and victimization in a national sample of higher education students. *Journal of Consulting and Clinical Psychology, 55,* 162–170.

Kuh, G. D. (2001). Assessing what really matters to student learning: Inside the National Survey of Student Engagement. *Change, 33*(3), 10–17.

Kuh, G. D. (2003). What we're learning about student engagement from NSSE. *Change, 35*(2), 24–32.

Kuh, G. D., Kinzie, J., Schuh, J. H., and Whitt, E. J. (2005). *Assessing conditions to enhance educational effectiveness: The inventory for student engagement and success.* San Francisco: Jossey-Bass.

LaBrie, J. W., and others. (2009). Preventing risky drinking in first-year college women: Further validation of a female-specific motivational-enhancement group intervention. *Journal of Studies on Alcohol and Drugs, Supplement No. 16,* 77–85.

Ladson-Billings, G. (2000). For colored girls who have considered suicide when the academy's not enough: Reflections of an African American woman scholar. In J. Glazer-Raymo, B. K. Townsend, and R. Ropers-Huilman (Eds.), *Women in higher education: A feminist perspective* (2nd ed., pp. 341–352). Boston: Pearson Custom Publishing.

Landry, D. E., and MacLean, G. (1993). *Materialist feminisms.* Oxford, UK: Blackwell Publishers.

Langdon, E. (2002). Extracurricular issues. In A. M. Martínez Alemán and K. A. Renn (Eds.), *Women in higher education* (pp. 302–306). Santa Barbara: ABC-CLIO.

Lapchick, R. (2009). *The 2008 racial and gender report card: College sport.* Orlando: University of Central Florida.

Lather, P. (1990). Reinscribing otherwise: The play of values in the practices of the human sciences. In E. Guba (Ed.), *The paradigm dialogue* (pp. 315–332). Newbury Park, CA: Sage.

Lather, P. (1991). *Getting smart: Feminist research with/in the postmodern.* New York: Routledge.

Lather, P. (1992). Critical frames in educational research: Feminist and post-structural perspectives. *Theory into Practice, 31*(2), 87–99.

Leonard, D. K., and Jiang, J. (1999). Gender bias and the college predictions of the SATs: A cry of despair. *Research in Higher Education, 40*(4), 375–407.

Lorde, A. (1984). *Sister outsider.* Berkeley, CA: Crossing Press.

Lovett, D. J., and Lowry, C. D. (1994). 'Good old boys' and 'good old girls' clubs: Myth or reality? *Journal of Sport Management, 8*(1), 27–35.

Lugones, M. C. (2003). *Pilgrimages/peregrinajes: A personal journey of resistance.* Oxford, UK: Rowman & Littlefield.

Lugones, M. C., and Spelman, E. V. (1983). Have we got a theory for you: Feminist theory, cultural imperialism and the demand for the woman's voice. *Women's Studies International Forum, 6*(6), 573–581.

Luna, A. L. (2006). Faculty salary equity cases: Combining statistics with the law. *Journal of Higher Education, 77*(2), 193–224.

Macdonald, B. J. (2002). Marx, Foucault, genealogy. *Polity, 34*(3), 259–284.

Maher, F. A., and Tetreault, M. K. (2002). Feminist pedagogy. In A. M. Martínez Alemán and K. A. Renn (Eds.), *Women in higher education* (pp. 130–135). Santa Barbara, CA: ABC-CLIO.

Marcus, J. (2007). Helping academics have families and tenure too: Universities discover their self-interest. *Change, 39*(2), 27–32.

Marschke, R., Laursen, S., Nielsen, J. M., and Rankin, P. (2007). Demographic inertia revisited: An immodest proposal to achieve equitable gender representation among faculty in higher education. *Journal of Higher Education, 78*(1), 1–26.

Marshall, C. (1999). Researching the margins: Feminist critical policy analysis. *Educational Policy, 13*(1), 18.

Marshall, C. (2000). Policy discourse analysis: Negotiating gender equity. *Journal of Education Policy, 15*(2), 32.

Martínez Alemán, A. M. (2008). Faculty productivity and the gender question. In J. Glazer-Raymo (Ed.). *Unfinished agendas: New and continuing gender challenges in higher education* (pp. 142–161). Baltimore: Johns Hopkins University Press.

Martínez Alemán, A. M., and Renn, K. A. (Eds.). (2002). *Women in higher education: An encyclopedia.* Santa Barbara, CA: ABC-CLIO.

Mason, M. A. (2009a, March 25). Do your job better. *Chronicle of Higher Education.* Retrieved May 1, 2010, from http://chronicle.com/article/Role-ModelsMentors/44794/.

Mason, M. A. (2009b, September). How the "snow-woman effect" slows women's progress. *The Chronicle of Higher Education.* Retrieved May 5, 2010, from http://chronicle.com/article/How-the-Snow-Woman-Effect/48377/.

Mason, M. A., and Goulden, M. (2004). Do babies matter (Part II)? Closing the baby gap. *Academe, 90*(6), 10–15.

Mason, M. A., Goulden, M., and Frasch, K. (2009). Why graduate students reject the fast track. *Academe, 95*(1), 11–16.

McCann, C., and Kim, S. (Eds.). (2003). *Feminist theory reader.* London, UK: Routledge.

McDonough, P. M. (2002). Resisting common injustice: Tenure politics, department politics, gay and lesbian politics. In J. E. Cooper and D. D. Stevens (Eds.), *Tenure in the sacred grove: Issues and strategies for women and minority faculty.* Albany: State University of New York Press.

McGuire, G. M., and Reger, J. (2003). Feminist co-mentoring: A model for academic professional development. *NWSA Journal, 15*(1), 54.

McIntosh, P. (1988). *White privilege and male privilege: A personal account of coming to see correspondences through work in women's studies* (Working Paper No. 189). Wellesley, MA: Center for Research on Women, Wellesley College.

McMahon, P. P. (2008). Sexual violence on the college campus: A template for compliance with federal policy. *Journal of American College Health, 57*(3), 361–366.

Messner, M. A., and Sabo, D. F. (Eds.). (1990). *Sport, men and the gender order: Critical feminist perspectives.* Champaign, IL: Human Kinetics.

Metcalfe, A. S., and Slaughter, S. (2008). The differential effects of academic capitalism on women in the academy. In J. Glazer-Raymo (Ed.), *Unfinished agendas: New and continuing gender challenges in higher education* (pp. 80–111). Baltimore: Johns Hopkins University Press.

Mies, M., and Shiva, V. (1993). *Ecofeminism.* London, UK: Zed Press.

Miller, C. D., and Kraus, M. (2004). Participating but not leading: Women's under-representation in student government leadership positions. *College Student Journal, 38*(3), 423–427.

Miller, P. (2008). The gender pay gap in the US: Does sector make a difference? *Journal of Labor Research, 30*(1), 52–74.

Millett, K. (1969). *Sexual politics.* New York: Doubleday.

Mohanty, C. T., Russo, A., and Torres, L. (Eds.). (1991). *Third World women and the politics of feminism.* Bloomington, IN: Indiana University Press.

Mohanty, C. T. (1991). Under Western eyes: Feminist scholarship and colonial discourses. In C. T. Mohanty, A. Russo, and L. Torres (Eds.), *Third world women and the politics of feminism* (pp. 51–80). Indianapolis: Indiana University Press.

Mohanty, C. T. (2003). *Feminism without borders: Decolonizing theory, practicing solidarity.* Durham, NC: Duke University Press.

Morris, L. K., and Daniel, L. G. (2008). Perceptions of a chilly climate: Differences in traditional and non-traditional majors for women. *Research in Higher Education, 49*(3), 256–273.

Mortenson, T. (2007). *Bachelor's degree attainment by age 24 by family income quartiles, 1970 to 2005.* Oskaloosa, IA: Postsecondary Education Opportunity.

Moses, Y. T. (2009). Advice from the field: Guiding women of color to academic leadership. In D. R. Dean, S. J. Bracken, and J. K. Allen (Eds.), *Women in academic leadership: Professional strategies, personal choices* (pp. 181–207). Sterling, VA: Stylus.

Narayan, U. (1997). Contesting cultures, 'Westernization,' Respect for cultures, and Third World feminists. In L. E. Nicholson (Ed.), *The second wave: A reader in feminist theory.* London, UK: Routledge.

Narayan, U. (2000). Essence of culture and sense of history: A feminist critique of cultural essentialism. In U. Narayan and S. Harding (Eds.), *Decentering the center: Philosophy for a multicultural, postcolonial, and feminist world* (pp. 80–100). Bloomington, IN: Indiana University Press.

National Coalition for Women and Girls in Education. (2002). *Title IX at 30: Report card on gender equity*. Washington, DC: National Coalition for Women and Girls in Education.

National Science Foundation, Division of Science Resource Statistics. (2007). *Women, minorities, and persons with disabilities in science and engineering: 2007* (NSF 07-315). Arlington, VA: National Science Foundation.

National Women's Studies Association. (2010). Web site. Retrieved September 10, 2010, from http://www.nwsa.org.

Nidiffer, J. (2000). *Pioneering deans of women: More than wise and pious matrons*. New York: Teachers College Press.

Nidiffer, J. (2001). New leadership for a new century: Women's contribution to leadership in higher education. In J. Nidiffer, and C. T. Bashaw (Eds.), *Women administrators in higher education* (pp. 101–131). Albany: State University of New York Press.

Nidiffer, J. (2002). Overview. In A. M. Martínez Alemán and K. A. Renn (Eds.), *Women in higher education* (pp. 3–15). Santa Barbara, CA: ABC-CLIO.

Nidiffer, J. (2010). Corrective lenses: Suffrage, feminist poststructural analysis, and the history of higher education. In E. J. Allan, S. V. Iverson, and R. Ropers-Huilman (Eds.), *Reconstructing policy in higher education: Feminist poststructural perspectives* (pp. 41–61). New York: Routledge.

Nidiffer, J., and Bashaw, C. T. (Eds.). (2001). *Women administrators in higher education: Historical and contemporary perspectives*. Albany: State University of New York Press.

Noble, D. F. (1992). *A world without women: The Christian clerical culture of Western science*. Oxford, UK: Oxford University Press.

Noddings, N. (1989). *Women and evil*. Berkeley: University of California Press.

Ohio State University. (1992). *The report of the president's commission on women*. Columbus: President's Commission on Women, Ohio State University.

Ohio State University, The Women's Place. (2010). Retrieved September 10, 2010, from http://womensplace.osu.edu/index.html.

Ortner, S. (1995). Resistance and the problem of ethnographic refusal. *Comparative Studies in Society and History, 37*, 173–193.

Pascarella, E. T., and Terenzini, P. T. (1991). *How college affects students: Findings and insights from twenty years of research*. San Francisco: Jossey-Bass.

Pascarella, E. T., and Terenzini, P. T. (2005). *How college affects students*. San Francisco: Jossey-Bass.

Pascarella, E. T., and others. (1997). Women's perceptions of a "chilly climate" and their cognitive outcomes during the first year of college. *Journal of College Student Development, 38*(2), 109–124.

Perna, L. (2002). Sex differences in the supplemental earnings of college and university faculty. *Research in Higher Education, 43*(1), 31–58.

Peterson, M. W., and Spencer, M. G. (1990). Understanding academic culture and climate. *New Directions for Institutional Research*, (No. 68, pp. 3–18). San Francisco: Jossey-Bass.

Pfeffer, J., and Ross, J. (1990). Gender-based wage differences: The effects of organizational context. *Work and Occupations, 17*(1), 55–78.

Pillow, W. S. (1997). Decentering silences/troubling irony: Teen pregnancy's challenge to policy analysis. In C. Marshall (Ed.), *Feminist critical policy analysis I: A perspective from primary and secondary schooling* (pp. 134–152). Washington, DC: Falmer Press.

Pillow, W. S. (2003). "Bodies are dangerous": Using feminist genealogy as policy studies methodology. *Journal of Education Policy, 18*(2), 5.

Porter, S. R., Toutkoushian, R. K., and Moore, J.V.I. (2008). Pay inequities for recently hired faculty, 1988–2004. *Review of Higher Education, 31*(4), 465–487.

Purcell, F. F. (2002). Women's studies. In A. M. Martínez Alemán and K. A. Renn (Eds.), *Women in higher education: An encyclopedia* (pp. 198–201). Santa Barbara, CA: ABC-CLIO.

Reichmuth, J. (2002). Sexual harassment. In A. M. Martínez Alemán and K. A. Renn (Eds.), *Women in higher education: An encyclopedia* (pp. 102–106). Santa Barbara, CA: ABC-CLIO.

Reinharz, S. (1992). *Feminist methods in social research*. Oxford, UK: Oxford University Press.

Rhoades, G. (2000). Who's doing it right? Strategic activity in public research universities. *Review of Higher Education, 24*(1), 26.

Rhoades, G., and Maitland, C. (1998). The hidden campus workforce: (De)investing in staff. In *NEA 1998 Almanac of Higher Education* (pp. 109–118). Washington, DC: National Education Association.

Rienzi, B. M., Allen, M. J., Sarmiento, Y. Q., and McMillin, J. D. (1993). Alumni perception of the impact of gender on their university experience. *Journal of College Student Development, 34*, 154–157.

Ropers-Huilman, R. (2000). Scholarship on the other side: Power and caring in feminist education. In J. Glazer-Raymo, B. K. Townsend, and R. Ropers-Huilman (Eds.), *Women in higher education: A feminist perspective* (2nd ed., pp. 546–557). Boston: Pearson Custom Publishing.

Ropers-Huilman, R. (2002). Overview. In A. M. Martínez Alemán and K. A. Renn (Eds.), *Women in higher education* (pp. 109–118). Santa Barbara, CA: ABC-CLIO.

Ropers-Huilman, R. (2003a). Gender in the future of higher education. In R. Ropers-Huilman (Ed.), *Gendered futures in higher education: Critical perspectives for change* (pp. 1–11). Albany: State University of New York Press.

Ropers-Huilman, R. (Ed.). (2003b). *Gendered futures in higher education: Critical perspectives for change*. Albany: State University of New York Press.

Ropers-Huilman, R., and Winters, K. T. (forthcoming). *Feminist research in higher education*. Manuscript accepted for publication in *The Journal of Higher Education*.

Rosenberg, R. (1982). Representing women at the state and local levels: Commissions on the status of women. In E. Boneparth (Ed.), *Women, power, and policy* (pp. 38–46). New York: Pergamon Press.

Rosenfeld, L. B., and Jarrard, M. W. (1985). The effects of perceived sexism in female and male college professors on students' descriptions of classroom climate. *Communication Education, 34*, 205–213.

Rosser, P. (1989). The SAT gender gap: Identifying the causes. Washington, DC: Center for Women Policy Studies.

Rosser, S. V. (1999). International experiences lead to using postcolonial feminism to transform life sciences curriculum. *Women's Studies International Forum, 22*(1), 3–15.

Rosser, S. V. (2004). *The science glass ceiling: Academic women scientists and the struggle to succeed.* New York: Routledge.

Rosser, S. V. (2007). Leveling the playing field for women in tenure and promotion. *NWSA Journal, 19*(3), 190–198.

Rosser, V. J. (2004). Faculty members' intentions to leave: A national study on their worklife and satisfaction. *Research in Higher Education, 45*(3), 285–309.

Rossi, A. S., and Calderwood, A. (1973). *Academic women on the move.* New York: Russell Sage Foundation.

Rothblum, E. D. (1988). Leaving the ivory tower: Factors contributing to women's voluntary resignation from academia. *Frontiers, 10*(2), 14–17.

Rowan-Kenyon, H. T. (2007). Predictors of delayed college enrollment and the impact of socioeconomic status. *Journal of Higher Education, 78*(2), 188–214.

Rubin, G. (1975). The traffic of women: Notes on the political economy of sex. In R. R. Reiter (Ed.), *Toward an anthropology of women* (pp. 157–210). New York: Monthly Review Press.

Sadker, D., Sadker, M., and Zittleman, K. R. (2009). *Still failing at fairness: How gender bias cheats girls and boys in school and what we can do about it.* New York: Scribner.

Sadker, M., and Sadker, D. (1995). *Failing at fairness: How our schools cheat girls.* New York: Touchstone.

Sagaria, M. D. (Ed.). (1988). *Empowering women: Leadership development strategies on campus* (Vol. 44). San Francisco: Jossey-Bass.

Sagaria, M. D. (2002). An exploratory model of filtering in administrative searches: Toward counter-hegemonic discourses. *Journal of Higher Education 73*(6), 677–710.

Sagaria, M. D. (2007a). Reframing gender equality initiatives as university adaptation. In M. D. Sagaria (Ed.), *Women, universities, and change: Gender equality in the European Union and the United States* (pp. 1–6). New York: Palgrave Macmillan.

Sagaria, M. D. (Ed.). (2007b). *Women, universities, and change: Gender equality in the European Union and the United States.* New York: Palgrave Macmillan.

Sagaria, M. D., and Rychener, M. A. (2002). Mobility. In A. M. Martínez Alemán and K. A. Renn (Eds.), *Women in higher education* (pp. 495–498). Santa Barbara, CA: ABC-CLIO.

Sagas, M., and Cunningham, G. B. (2004). Does having "the right stuff" matter? Gender differences in the determinants of career success among intercollegiate athletic administrators. *Sex Roles, 50*(5–6), 411–421.

Sagas, M., Cunningham, G. B., and Teed, K. (2006). An examination of homologous reproduction in the representation of assistant coaches of women's teams. *Sex Roles, 55*(7–8), 503–510.

Salter, D. W. (2003). Exploring the "chilly classroom" phenomenon as interactions between psychological and environmental types. *Journal of College Student Development, 44*(1), 110–121.

Sander, L. (2009, February 19). Racial and gender diversity in college sports is "worse" in many years, report says. *Chronicle of Higher Education.* Retrieved June 1, 2010, from http://chronicle.com.

Sandler, B. R., Silverberg, L., and Hall, R. M. (1996). *The chilly classroom climate: A guide to improve the education of women.* Washington, DC: National Association of Women in Education.

Santovec, M. L. (2007). Tips to use mentoring and mapping to advance a career. *Women in Higher Education 16*(10), 2.

Sax, L. J., and Harper, C. (2007). Origins of the gender gap: Pre-college and college influences on the differences between men and women. *Research in Higher Education, 48*(6), 669–694.

Scherer Hawthorne, L. (2002). Sexual assault. In A. M. Martínez Alemán and K. A. Renn (Eds.), *Women in higher education: An encyclopedia* (pp. 350–352). Santa Barbara, CA: ABC-CLIO.

Scheurich, J. J. (1994). Policy archaeology: A new policy studies methodology. *Journal of Education Policy, 9*(4), 20.

Schiebinger, L. (2004). *Nature's body: Gender in the making of modern science.* Rutgers, NJ: Rutgers University Press.

Schonberger, A. K. (2002). Overview. In A. M. Martínez Alemán and K. A. Renn (Eds.), *Women in higher education: An Encyclopedia* (pp. 143–155). Santa Barbara, CA: ABC-CLIO.

Schwartz, M. (2006). Voices of women in the field: I'm glad no one told me . . . . *Journal of Women in Educational Leadership, 4*(4), 265–267.

Schwartz, M., and Akins, L. (2004). *Policies, practices, and composition of governing boards of independent colleges and universities.* Washington, DC: Association of Governing Boards.

Scott, J. (1988). Deconstructing equality versus difference: Or, the uses of post-structuralist theory for feminism. *Feminist Studies, 14*(1), 18.

Scott, R. A. (1978). *Lords, squires, and yeomen: Collegiate middle managers and their organizations* (Report No. 7). Washington, DC: American Association for Higher Education.

Serex, C. P., and Townsend, B. K. (1999). Student perceptions of chilling practices in sex-atypical majors. *Research in Higher Education, 40*(5), 527–538.

Shaw, I. S. (2007). Issues after tenure. *National Women's Studies Association Journal, 19*(3), 7–14.

Slaughter, S., and Leslie, L. (1997). *Academic capitalism: Politics, policies, and the entrepreneurial university.* Baltimore: Johns Hopkins University Press.

Slaughter, S., and Rhoades, G. (2004). *Academic capitalism and the new economy: Markets, state, and higher education.* Baltimore: Johns Hopkins University Press.

Sloma-Williams, L., McDade, S. A., Richman, R. C., and Morahan, P. S. (2009). The role of self-efficacy in developing women leaders: A case of women in academic medicine and dentistry. In D. R. Dean, S. J. Bracken, and J. K. Allen (Eds.), *Women in academic leadership: Professional strategies, personal choices* (pp. 50–73). Sterling, VA: Stylus.

Smith, D. E. (1990). *The conceptual practices of power: A feminist sociology of knowledge.* Boston: Northeastern University Press.

Smith, L. T. (1999). *Decolonizing methodologies.* New York: Zed Books.

Snyder, T. D., and Dillow, S. A. (2010). *Digest of Educational Statistics 2009.* Washington, DC: National Center for Education Statistics.

Snyder, T. D., Dillow, S. A., and Hoffman, C. M. (2008). *Digest of Education Statistics, 2007.* Washington, DC: National Center for Education Statistics.

Snyder, T. D., Dillow, S. A., and Hoffman, C. M. (2009). *Digest of Education Statistics, 2008.* Washington, DC: National Center for Education Statistics.

Snyder, T. D., Tan, A. G., and Hoffman, C. M. (2006). *Digest of Education Statistics 2005.* Washington, DC: National Center for Education Statistics.

Solomon, B. M. (1985). *In the company of educated women: A history of women and higher education in America.* New Haven, CT: Yale University Press.

Somers, P. (2002). Title IX. In A. M. Martínez Alemán and K. A. Renn (Eds.), *Women in higher education* (pp. 237–244). Santa Barbara, CA: ABC-CLIO.

Stack, S. (2004). Gender, children and research productivity. *Research in Higher Education, 45*(8), 891–920.

Stage, F. K., and Hubbard, S. (2008). Developing women scientists: Baccalaureate origins of recent mathematics and science doctorates. In J. Glazer-Raymo (Ed.), *Unfinished agendas: New and continuing gender challenges in higher education* (pp. 112–141). Baltimore: Johns Hopkins University Press.

Stangl, J. M., and Kane, M. J. (1991). Structural variables that offer explanatory power for the underrepresentation of women coaches since Title IX: The case of homologous reproduction. *Sociology of Sport Journal, 8*(1), 47–60.

Starhawk. (1979). *The spiral dance.* San Francisco: Harper & Row.

Starhawk. (1989). Feminist earth-based spirituality and ecofeminism. In J. Plant (Ed.), *Healing the wounds: The promise of ecofeminism* (pp. 174–185). Santa Cruz, CA: New Society Publishers.

Starhawk. (2002). *Webs of power: Notes from the global uprising.* Gabriola, BC: New Society Publishers.

Stewart, D. W. (1980). *The women's movement in community politics in the U.S.: The role of local commissions on the status of women.* New York: Pergamon Press.

Stone, D. (2002). *The art of political decision making.* New York: Norton & Company.

Stout, P. A., Staiger, J., and Jennings, N. A. (2007). Affective stories: Understanding the lack of progress of women faculty. *NWSA Journal, 19*(3), 124–144.

Stromquist, N. P. (2006). Women's rights to adult education as a means to citizenship. *International Journal of Educational Development, 26*(2), 140–152.

Stromquist, N. P. (2007). *Gender equity education globally* (2nd ed.). Mahwah, NJ: Lawrence Erlbaum.

Stromquist, N. P. (2010). Knowledge capital and excellence: Implications of a science-centered university for gender equity. In E. J. Allan, S. V. Iverson, and R. Ropers-Huilman (Eds.), *Reconstructing policy in higher education: Feminist poststructural perspectives* (pp. 215–234). New York: Routledge.

Suggs, W. (2008). *A place on the team: The triumph and tragedy of Title IX.* Princeton, NJ: Princeton University Press.

Taylor, K., and Marienau, C. (2008). Effective practices in fostering developmental growth in women learners. In J. Allen, S. J. Bracken, and D. Dean (Eds.), *Most college students are women: Implications for teaching, learning, and policy* (pp. 55–74). Sterling, VA: Stylus.

Taylor, H. (1851, July). Enfranchisement of women. *Westminster and Foreign Quarterly Review.*

The Women's Place at The Ohio State University. (2010). *Mission, vision, and guiding principles.* Retrieved from http://womensplace.osu.edu/mission-vision-and-guiding-principles.html.

Tierney, W. G. (1997). Organizational socialization in higher education. *Journal of Higher Education, 68*(1), 1–16.

Tong, R. (2009). *Feminist thought: A more comprehensive introduction.* Boulder, CO: Westview Press.

Touchton, J., Musil, C. T., and Campbell, K. P. (2008). *A measure of equity: Women's progress in higher education.* Washington, DC: Association of American Colleges and Universities.

Toutkoushian, R. K. (2003). Addressing gender equity in nonfaculty salaries. *New Directions for Institutional Research, 2003*(117), 49–68.

Toutkoushian, R. K., Bellas, M. L., and Moore, J. V. (2007). The interaction effects of gender, race, and marital status on faculty salaries. *Journal of Higher Education, 78*(5), 572–601.

Trower, C. A., and Bleak, J. L. (2004). *The study of new scholars. Gender: Statistical report [universities].* Cambridge, MA: Harvard Graduate School of Education.

Turner, C.S.V. (2002). Women of color in academe: Living with multiple marginality. *Journal of Higher Education, 73*(1), 74–93.

Turner, C.S.V. (2003). Incorporation and marginalization in the academy: From border toward center for faculty of color? *Journal of Black Studies, 34*, 112–125.

Turner, C.S.V. (2008). Women of color in academe: Experiences of the often invisible. In J. Glazer-Raymo (Ed.), *Unfinished agendas: New and continuing gender challenges in higher education* (pp. 230–252). Baltimore: Johns Hopkins University Press.

Turner, C. S., and Kappes, J. (2009). Preparing women of color for leadership: Perspectives on the American Council on Education (ACE) fellows program. In D. R. Dean, S. J. Bracken, and J. K. Allen. (Eds.), *Women in academic leadership: Professional strategies, personal choices* (pp. 149–180). Sterling, VA: Stylus.

Umbach, P. (2007). Gender equity in the academic labor market: An analysis of academic disciplines. *Research in Higher Education, 48*(2), 169–192.

Valian, V. (1999). *Why so slow? The advancement of women.* Cambridge, MA: MIT Press.

Vander Hooven, J. L. (2009). *Lessons from success: The experiences of women who completed an associate degree while parenting children.* Doctoral dissertation. Retrieved September 20, 2010, from http://proquest.umi.com.

Walby, S. (1986). *Patriarchy at work: Patriarchal and capitalist relations in employment.* Minneapolis: University of Minnesota Press.

Walker, A. (1983). In search of our mothers' gardens: Womanist prose. New York: Harcourt Brace Jovanovich.

Ward, K., and Bensimon, E. (2002). Socialization. In A. M. Martínez Alemán, and K. A. Renn, (Eds.), *Women in higher education: An encyclopedia.* Santa Barbara: ABC-CLIO, pp. 431–434.

Women's Status in Higher Education

Ward, K., and Wolf-Wendel, L. (2004). Fear factor: How safe is it to make time for family? *Academe, 90*, 28–31.

Ward, K., and Wolf-Wendel, L. (2008). Choice and discourse in faculty careers: Feminist perspectives on work and family. In Glazer-Raymo, J. (Ed)., *Unfinished agendas: New and continuing challenges in higher education*, (pp. 253–272). Baltimore: Johns Hopkins University Press.

Warren, K. J. (2000). *Ecofeminist philosophy, a western perspective on what it is and why it matters*. Lanham, MD: Rowman & Littlefield.

Warshaw, R. (1994). *I never called it rape: The* Ms. *report on recognizing, fighting and surviving date and acquaintance rape*. New York: Harper & Row.

Wasburn, M. H. (2007). Mentoring women faculty: An instrumental case study of strategic collaboration. *Mentoring & Tutoring: Partnership in Learning, 15*(1), 57–72.

Webber, K., and Lee, K. *Factors Related to Faculty Productivity: Evidence from NSOPF:2004*. Scholarly Paper presented at the Association for the Study of Higher Education conference, November, 2009, Vancouver, BC.

Webster, B. H., and Bishaw, A. (2007). *Income, earnings, and poverty data from the 2006 American community survey*. U.S. Department of Commerce. https://www.census.gov/prod/2007pubs/acs-08.pdf

Weedon, C. (1999). *Feminism, theory and the politics of difference*. Boston: Blackwell Publishers.

West, C., and Fenstermaker, S. (1995). Doing difference. *Gender & Society, 91*, 3–37.

West, M. S., and Curtis, J. W. (2006). *AAUP faculty gender equity indicators, 2006*. Washington, DC: American Association of University Professors.

White, J. S. (2005). Pipeline to pathways: New directions for improving the status of women on campus. *Liberal Education, 91*(1), 22–27.

Whitt, E. J. (1993). *"I can be anything!": Student leadership in three women's colleges*. Paper presented at the annual meeting of the Association for the Study of Higher Education, November, Pittsburgh, PA.

Whitt, E. J., and others. (1999). Women's perceptions of a "chilly climate" and cognitive outcomes in college: Additional evidence. *Journal of College Student Development, 40*(2), 163–177.

Williams, J. (2000). How the tenure track discriminates against women. *Chronicle of Higher Education, 60*(1), 59–82.

Williams, P. J. (1991). *The alchemy of race and rights: Diary of a law professor*. Cambridge, MA: Harvard University Press.

Williams, P. J. (1997). Spirit-murdering the messenger: The discourse of fingerpointing as the law's response to racism. In A. K. Wing (Ed.), *Critical race feminism: A reader* (pp. 229–236). New York: New York University Press.

Wilson, J. Q. (1973). *Political organizations*. New York: Basic Books.

Wilson, R. (2004, December). Where the elite teach, it's still a man's world. *The Chronicle of Higher Education, 51*(15), A8.

Winston, K., and Bane, M. J. (Eds.). (1993). *Gender and public policy: Cases and comments*. Boulder, CO: Westview Press.

Wolf-Wendel, L., and Ward, K. (2003). Future prospects for women faculty: Negotiating work and family. In R. Ropers-Huilman (Ed.), *Gendered futures in higher education: Critical perspectives for change* (pp. 111–134). Albany: State University of New York Press.

Wolf-Wendel, L., and Ward, K. (2006a). Academic life and motherhood: Variations by institutional type. *Higher Education, 52*(3), 487–521.

Wolf-Wendel, L., and Ward, K. (2006b). Faculty work and family life: Policy perspectives from different institutional types. In S. J. Bracken, J. K. Allen, and D. R. Dean (Eds.), *The balancing act: Gendered perspectives in faculty roles and work lives* (pp. 51–72). Sterling, VA: Stylus.

Wolf-Wendel, L., Ward, K., and Twombly, S. B. (2007). Faculty life at community colleges: The perspective of women with children. *Community College Review, 34*(4), 255–281.

Women in Higher Education. (2010). Homepage. Retrieved May 1, 2010, from http://www.wihe.com/.

Young, I. M. (1990). *Justice and the politics of difference.* Princeton, NJ: Princeton University Press.

Zamani, E. M. (2003). African American women in higher education. In M. F. Howard-Hamilton (Ed.), *New directions for student services* (Vol. 104, pp. 5–18). San Francisco, CA: Jossey-Bass.

Name Index

A

Acosta, R. V., 48, 49, 56, 57, 59, 63
Adair, V. C., 87
Adams, A., 21
Adelman, C., 39, 66
Ahern, D. W., 9, 103
Aisenberg, N., 10
Allan, E. J., 15, 16, 30, 37, 49, 69, 83, 84, 100, 106, 107, 112, 113, 123
Allen, A., 19, 20, 22, 24, 27
Allen, J. K., 94, 124
Allen, M. J., 68
Allen, W. R., 66
Altman, M., 108
Amey, M. J., 82, 83
Andberg, W. L., 68
Anderson, D. J., 49, 50
Anzaldua, G., 26
Asher, N., 122
Astin, A. W., 68
Astin, H. S., 47, 82
Atkins, L., 62
August, L., 77

B

Bacchi, C. L., 15, 105, 106
Bailey, T. M., 43
Ball, S. J., 106
Bandura, A., 70
Bane, M. J., 106
Banks, T., 68
Bartkowski, F., 19, 20, 21
Bashaw, C. T., 82
Basow, S., 86
Baxter, J., 29, 30
Becker, W. E., 89
Belenky, M. F., 29
Bellas, M. L., 54, 89
Bensimon, E. M., 30, 80, 82, 83, 105, 106, 123
Berry, T. R., 87
Birnbaum, R., 83
Bishaw, A., 43, 44
Blackmore, J., 106
Bleak, J., 77
Blickenstaff, J. C., 86
Bok, D., 52
Bornstein, R., 2, 60, 82, 85, 111
Bowen, H. R., 76
Bracken, S. J., 94, 124
Brady, K. L., 69
Bratt, C. S., 61
Broad, M., 60
Brooks, V. R., 68
Brown, H., 61
Bryson, M., 15, 106, 123
Bunch, C., 16, 26
Burton, L., 59
Butler, J., 30

C

Calderwood, A., 7, 10
Campbell, K. P., 2, 10, 38, 39, 43, 44, 51, 53, 58, 59, 60, 63, 89

Carducci, R., 83
Carpenter, L. J., 48, 49, 56, 57, 59, 63
Carter, D. F., 66
Chamberlain, M. K., 4, 10
Cheslock, J. J., 49, 50
Chism, N. V., 67
Chliwniak, L., 82
Chodorow, N., 28
Christ, C., 27
Cixous, H., 28, 30
Clayton-Pedersen, A. R., 66
Clinchy, B. M., 29
Coleman, M. S., 61
Collins, P. H., 26, 87, 106, 117
Constantinople, A., 68
Contreras-McGavin, M., 83
Conway, M. M., 9, 103
Cook, B. J., 44, 59, 60, 63
Cook, D., 111
Cook, J. A., 116
Cook, S. G., 102
Cooper, J., 54
Cooper, J. E., 2, 11, 62, 87
Corbett, C., 39, 40, 41
Cordova, D. I., 44, 59, 60, 63
Cornelius, R., 68
Coser, L. A., 80
Cox, E. M., 2, 82, 85
Crawford, M., 68
Crenshaw, K., 26
Cress, C., 13, 66, 78
Cullen, F. T., 9, 72, 73
Cunningham, G. B., 59
Curtis, J. W., 38, 40, 52, 89

D

Dahlberg, S. L., 87
Daly, M., 23, 27
Daniel, L. G., 70
Davis, F., 103
De Castell, S., 15, 106, 123
De Lauretis, T., 28
Dean, D. R., 94, 107, 109, 124
Dillow, S. A., 2, 3, 38, 39, 43, 44, 52, 53, 63
Dinnerstein, D., 27, 28

Dominici, F., 58
Donovan, J., 20, 21
Drago, R., 114
Drew, T. L., 68

E

Eckes, S. E., 114
Eddy, P. L., 2, 60, 80, 81, 82, 83, 85
Ehrenberg, R. G., 49, 50
Eisenhart, M., 68, 74, 75
Eisenstein, Z., 24
Eisler, R. M., 69
Enloe, C., 26
Estler, S. E., 49, 57

F

Evers, F., 41, 46
Faust, D. G., 61
Fellabaum, J., 13
Ferree, M. M., 89
Festle, M. J., 49
Fine, M., 106
Firestone, S., 23, 28
Fisher, B. S., 9, 72, 73
Flax, J., 28
Follet, C. V., 68
Fonow, M. M., 116
Ford, J., 83
Foster, M. S., 68
Foster, T. J., 68
Foucault, M., 29
Frankenberg, R., 88
Frasch, K., 2, 46, 80, 81, 86
Fraser, N., 106
Freeman, J., 7
French, M., 23
Fried, L. P., 58
Friedan, B., 21, 28
Fuss, Diana, 28

G

Gidycz, C. A., 72
Gilligan, C., 28, 29
Gilmartin, S. K., 75
Glazer-Raymo, J., 2, 7, 10, 15, 17, 48, 49, 52, 61, 63, 82, 83, 99, 103, 105, 121, 123

Rowan-Kenyon, H. T., 40
Rubin, G., 23
Russo, A., 117
Rychener, M. A., 110

S

Sabo, D. F., 57
Sax, L. J., 43
Sadker, D., 40
Sadker, M., 40
Sagaria, M. D., 17, 82, 88, 109, 110, 115
Sagas, M., 59
St. Pierre, E., 30
St. Rose, A., 39, 40, 41
Salter, D. W., 68
Sander, L., 50
Sandler, B., 101
Sandler, B. R., 2, 8, 10, 67, 68
Santovec, M. L., 111
Sarmiento, Y. Q., 68
Sax, L. J., 75
Scherer Hawthorne, L., 73
Scheurich, J. J., 106
Schiebinger, L., 87
Schonberger, A. K., 9, 116
Schuh, J. H., 70
Schuster, J. H., 76
Schwartz, M., 62, 77
Scollay, S. J., 61
Scott, J., 30
Scott, R. A., 76
Sears, A., 77–78
Serex, C. P., 69
Shaw, I. S., 54
Shiva, V., 27, 28
Silva, E., 73
Silverberg, L., 2, 67, 68
Simmons, R., 61
Simon, L. A., 61
Slaughter, S., 114
Sloma-Williams, L., 112
Smith, D. E., 106
Smith, L. T., 87
Snyder, T. D., 2, 3, 38, 39, 43, 44, 52, 53, 54, 63
Solomon, B. M., 4, 5

Somers, P., 8
Spelman, E. V., 17, 26
Spencer, M. G., 13
Stack, S., 81
Stage, F. K., 86
Staiger, J., 9, 78
Stangl, J. M., 59
Starhawk, 27
Steuernagel, G. A., 9, 103
Stevens, D. D., 2, 62, 87
Stewart, D. W., 6, 7
Stone, D., 106
Stout, P. A., 9, 78
Stromquist, N. P., 122
Suggs, W., 49

T

Tan, A. G., 54
Tarule, J. M., 29
Taylor, H., 20, 21
Taylor, K., 75
Taylor, L., 66
Teed, K., 59
Terenzini, P. T., 47, 71
Tetreault, M. K., 116, 117
Thompson, C., 28
Tickamyer, A. R., 61
Tierney, W. G., 66
Tilghman, S., 61
Tong, R., 18, 19, 20, 21, 22, 23, 24, 25, 26, 28, 31, 97
Torres, L., 117
Touchton, J., 2, 10, 38, 39, 43, 44, 51, 53, 58, 59, 60, 63, 89
Toutkoushian, R. K., 89, 90, 114
Townsend, B. K., 10, 17, 69
Trower, C., 77
Turner, C. S., 110, 111
Turner, M. T., 9, 72, 73, 87, 88
Twombly, S. B., 82, 83

U

Umbach, P., 89

V

Valian, V., 2, 17, 47, 52, 79, 81, 85, 108, 109, 115

Vander Hooven, J. L., 47
VanDerLinden, K. E., 83

W

Walby, S., 25
Walker, A., 26, 117
Walter, A., 66
Waltman, J., 77
Ward, K. B., 79, 80, 81, 82
Warren, K. J., 27, 28
Warshaw, R., 73
Wasburn, M. H., 107, 108
Webber, K., 81
Webster, B. H., 43, 44
Weedon, C., 30
Welch, V., Jr., 50
West, M. S., 38, 40, 52, 89
White, J. S., 91
Whitmore, R. W., 54

Whitt, E. J., 68, 70, 71
Williams, K., 50
Williams, P. J., 106
Wilson, J. Q., 100
Wilson, R., 65, 78
Winston, K., 106
Winters, K. T., 121
Wisniewski, N., 72
Wolf-Wendel, L., 79, 80, 81, 82
Wollstonecraft, M., 20, 21
Work, G. G., 68
Yamada, M., 26
Young, I. M., 25

Z

Zamani, E. M., 87
Zeger, S. L., 58
Zittleman, K. R., 40

Subject Index

A

AAUW Educational Foundation, 74

"Academic capitalism," 114

Access: women getting into college indicator of, 38–39; of women to educational quality, 40–41; of women to exclusive higher education institutions, 41–42. *See also* Representation

Activism strategies, 99–102

Affirmative Action Offices, 112

Alice Manicur Women's Symposium, 110

American Association of State Colleges and Universities, 110

American Association of University Professors, 7, 38, 88–89

American Association of University Women, 40, 41, 73

American Council on Education (ACE), 11, 60, 101, 111, 123

American Federation of Teachers, 52, 55

American Professors: A National Resource Imperiled (Bowen and Schuster), 76

American Psychological Association, 74

Association of American Colleges and Universities (AACU), 10, 101

Association of Governing Boards (AGB), 61, 62

Athletics department: cocurricular involvement in, 48–50; Title IX (Education Amendments) impact on, 8, 21, 37, 48–50, 57, 98–99, 103, 104*e*; women athletics directors of, 58–59;

women staff working in, 56–57. *See also* Division I institutions

B

Bell, Grove City v., 105*e*

Black feminism, 117

Black Feminist Thought (Collins), 117

C

Campus climate: assessing attainment of equity using, 65–67; campus safety and, 72–74; equity and classroom climate, 67–70; "romance culture" of, 74–75; salary equity and, 88–90, 114; student engagement and cocurricular leadership and, 70–72; for women staff, faculty, and administrators, 75–88. *See also* Institutions

Campus Compact, 48

Campus safety, 72–74

Campus Women Lead, On Campus with Women (newsletter), 101

Center for the Education of Women (University of Michigan), 77

Center for Policy Analysis, 11

Center for Public Integrity, 73

Center for Women and Leadership Faculty Fellows (Loyola University), 110

Change strategies. *See* Women's status change strategies

"Chilly classroom climate," 67–69, 86

The Chronicle of Higher Education, 65, 84

Civil Rights Act (1964), 7–8, 104*e*
Civil Rights Restoration Act (1987/1988), 105*e*
Classroom climate, 67–70
Cocurricular representation: athletics, 48–50; campus climate and leadership, 70–72; student leadership, 47–48
Collaborative on Academic Careers in Higher Education (COACHE), 78
College presidents, 59–61
College Student Experiences Questionnaire, 68
Committee for the Equality of Women (Harvard University), 102
Committee W (AAUP), 7
Committee on Women in the Academic Profession (Committee W), 101
Curriculum: promoting gender equity by transformation of, 115–117; women's contributions to, 8–9

D
Decentering the Center: Philosophy for a Multicultural, Postcolonial, and Feminist World (Narayan), 117
Declaration of Sentiments and Resolutions (1848), 5
Division I institutions: Title IX compliance among, 49–50; women athletics directors in, 59. *See also* Athletics department
Drawing the Line (Hill and Silva), 74

E
Ecofeminism, 27–28, 96*e*
Ecofeminist Philosophy: A Western Perspective on What It Is and Why It Matters (Warren), 28
Educated in Romance: Women, Achievement, and College Culture (Holland and Eisenhart), 74
Education Amendments (1972), 8
Educational quality access, 40–42
Equal Employment Opportunity (EEO), 112
Equal Pay Act (1963), 7, 103, 104*e*, 113–114

Equal Rights Amendment (ERA), 6
Ethnicity. *See* Racial/ethnic differences
Executive Order 11246, 104*e*

F
Faculty: family balance by, 79–82; gender differences among, 52–55; gender differences in satisfaction of, 78; percentage of full-time female faculty by discipline, 54*fig*; percentage of women faculty by institutional type, 52–53*fig*; racial/ethnic differences in satisfaction of, 78; salary equity issue and, 88–90, 114
Fair Labor Standards Act, 104*e*
Family balance, 79–82
Family and Medical Leave Act (1993), 105*e*
"Femi-Nazis," 18
Feminist Majority Foundation, 11
Feminist Organizations and Social Transformation in Latin America (Stromquist), 122
Feminist pedagogy, 116–117
Feminist Research in Higher Education (Ropers-Huilman and Winters), 121
Feminist theories: black, 117; comparison of multiple frames of, 19–31; ecofeminism, 27–28, 96*e*; enhancing gender equity strategies in context of, 94–98; implications of, 121–124; liberal feminism, 20–22, 91–92, 95*e*, 98; Marxist, socialist, and materialist, 24–25, 95*e*, 114–115; multicultural, global, and postcolonial, 25–26, 96*e*; postmodern, poststructural, and third wave, 29–31, 97*t*; psychological feminism, 28–29, 92, 97*e*; radical feminism, 22–24, 92, 95*e*, 121–122; range of, 18–19; recommendations for practice using, 124–125; suited to examine gender equity, 17–18. *See also* Gender equity; Theories; Women's status
Freud's theories, 28

G
Gender differences: athletics and, 48–50; campus safety, sexual assault and

K

Knowledge Capital and Excellence: Implications of a Science-Centered University for Gender Equity (Stromquist), 122

Knowledge production, 115–117

L

Leadership: campus climate and faculty/staff, 82–85; enhancing gender equity by promoting women's, 109–112; gender equity strategies to increase women's, 109–112; student, 47–48, 70–72; "surplus visibility" phenomenon of female, 85; women administrators and, 57–58, 76–90, 114. *See also* Professional development

Legislation: Civil Rights Act (1964), 7–8, 104e; Civil Rights Restoration Act (1987/1988), 105e; Education Amendments (1972), 8; Equal Pay Act (1963), 7, 103, 104e, 113–114; Equal Rights Amendment (ERA), 6; Fair Labor Standards Act, 104e; Family and Medical Leave Act (1993), 105e; Morrill Act (1862), 5; Nineteenth Amendment (1920), 5, 103; Pregnancy Discrimination Act (1978), 105e; Public Health Services Act (1975), 104e; Title IX (Education Amendments), 8, 21, 37, 48–50, 57, 98–99, 103, 104e; Title VII (Civil Rights Act), 7–8, 37, 103; Vocational Education Act Amendment (1976), 104e; Women's Educational Equity Act (1974), 104e. *See also* Public policy initiatives

Letters on Equality (Grimké), 21

Liberal feminism, 20–22, 91–92, 95e, 98

Lords, Squires, and Yeoman: Collegiate Middle Managers and Their Organizations (Scott), 76

Loyola University, 110

M

Marxist feminism, 24–25

Materialist Feminism: A Reader in Class,

Difference, and Women's Lives (Hennessy and Ingraham), 25

Materialist feminism, 24–25

Materialist Feminism and the Politics of Difference (Hennessey), 25

A Measure of Equity: Women's Progress in Higher Education (Touchton, Musil, and Campbell), 10

Mentoring: different types of, 108; enhancing gender equity through, 107–109; "grooming," 108; professional development through, 107–110

Meridians: Feminism, Race, and Transnationalism (journal), 117

Millennium Leadership Initiative, 110

Morrill Act (1862), 5

Multicultural feminism, 25–26, 96e

N

NASPA, 110, 111

National Coalition for Women and Girls in Education, 40

National Education Longitudinal Study, 40

National Hispanic Leadership Institute, 110

National Institute for Leadership Development, 110

National Organization for Women, 8, 21

National Science Foundation, 45, 86

National Survey of Student Engagement, 48, 70

National Women's Studies Association, 116, 123

Networking strategies, 99–102

"New Basics" curriculum, 39

Nineteenth Amendment (1920), 5, 103

O

Oedipus complex, 28, 29

Office of Women in Higher Education, 101

Ohio State University, 37, 65, 113

Old boy network, 59, 60–61

Olympe de Gouges (France), 21

"On the Equality of the Sexes" (1791), 21

Organizing strategies, 99–102

P

Patsy T. Mink Equal Opportunity in Education Act (2002), 8
Pedagogical strategies, 115–117
"Penis envy," 28
Postcolonial feminism, 25–26, 96e
Postmodern feminism, 29–31, 97e
Poststructural feminism, 30–31, 97e
Pregnancy Discrimination Act (1978), 105e
Presidential Commission on the Status of Women, 6, 7
Professional development: enhancing gender leadership through, 109–112; mentoring approach to, 107–110. *See also* Leadership
Program on the Status and Education of Women, 101
Project on the Status and Education of Women, 10
Psychological feminism, 28–29, 92, 97e
Public Health Services Act (1975), 104e
Public policy initiatives: key initiatives shaping women's status, 7–8, 104e–105e; promoting gender equity through, 102–103, 105–107. *See also* Legislation

R

Racial/ethnic differences: classroom climate and, 69–70; female college and university presidents, 59; gaps amplified for women of color, 63; in satisfaction by faculty, 78; in self-perceived leadership skills, 71–72; women doctoral recipients and, 50, 51*fig*. *See also* Women of color
Radical feminism, 22–24, 92, 95e, 121–122
Radical-cultural feminism, 22–23
Radical-libertarian feminism, 22–23
Rape, 72–74
Representation: enrollment of women in higher education, 42–44; female faculty, 52–55; female graduate students, 50–51*fig*; scholarship examination of issue of, 37–38; women in athletics,

48–50; of women degree earners, 44–47; women and governing boards, 61–62; women staff in higher education, 55–61; women in student leadership, 47–48. *See also* Access
Research in Higher Education, 93
Review of Higher Education, 93
"Romance culture," 74–75

S

Sage: A Scholarly Journal of Black Women, 117
Salary equity, 88–90, 114
San Diego State University, 116
Seneca Falls Convention (1848), 5
Senior administrators: campus climate for female, 75–88; family balance by, 79–82; leadership of female, 82–85; salary equity of, 88–90, 114; women in positions as, 57–58; work life satisfaction of female, 76–79
Sexual assault, 72–74
"Sexual auction block," 75
Sexual harassment reports, 74
Sexual identity, 87
Shattering the Myths: Women in Academe (Glazer-Raymo), 10
Socialist feminism, 24–25, 95e, 114–115
Spectrum Initiative, 111
Staff. *See* Women staff
"Stall-out" problem, 54–55
Staying Competitive: Patching America's Leaky Pipeline in the Sciences (Goulden, Frasch, and Mason), 86
STEM fields: mentoring and professional development in, 107; research on women faculty in, 86–87, 122; women and degree attainment in, 45–47
"Sticky floor" problem, 56
Student engagement: campus climate, leadership, and, 70–72; classroom climate and, 67–70
Student leadership: campus climate and, 70–72; gender differences in perceived, 71–72; representation of women in, 47–48

personnel, 56*fig*; salary equity and, 88–90, 114; senior administrators, 57–58; work life satisfaction of, 76–79

Women students: academic life aspects dissuading graduate studies by, 77–78; access to educational quality, 40–42; access to postsecondary education, 38–39; athletics representation among, 48–50; degree attainment by, 44–47; enrollment rates of, 42–44; graduate education of, 50–51*fig*; leadership skills perceived by, 71–72; sexual assault and harassment of, 72–74; STEM degree attainment by, 45–47; student leadership by, 47–48. *See also* Gender differences

Women, Universities and Change: Gender Equality in the European Union and the United States, 11

Women's Bureau (Department of Labor), 7

Women's Educational Equity Act (1974), 104*e*

Women's Equity Action League, 8

Women's Place (Ohio State University), 113

Women's status: events advancing and shaping, 1; examining the current state of, 1–2; guiding assumptions and questions about, 3–4; historical context of, 4–7; key policy initiatives shaping, 7–8, 104*e*–105*e*; recommendations for further research on, 119–120; recommendations for practices promoting, 124–125; strategies for advancing, 93–117; theoretical frameworks to examine, 16–35. *See also* Feminist theories; Gender equity; Higher education

Women's status change strategies: for enhancing gender equity, 98–117; for increasing women leadership, 109–112; mentoring as, 107–109; multiple feminist frames for, 94, 95*e*–97*e*; organizing schemes for, 94–98; public policy initiatives used as, 102–107; recommendations for practice of feminism in, 124–125

Work life satisfaction, 76–79

World Bank, 122

About the Author

Elizabeth J. Allan is professor of higher education at the University of Maine. She received her Ph.D. in educational policy and leadership with an emphasis on women's studies from Ohio State University. Her research focuses on campus cultures and climates and has included studies on campus diversity, university women's commissions, teaching practices, the methodology of policy discourse analysis, and student hazing. She has published more than twenty-five articles and chapters and is the recipient of the Outstanding Publication Award by the American Educational Research Association's Division J. She also is the author of *Policy Discourses, Gender, and Education* (2008) and coeditor of *Reconstructing Higher Education: Feminist Poststructural Perspectives* (2010).

About the ASHE Higher Education Report Series

Since 1983, the ASHE (formerly ASHE-ERIC) Higher Education Report Series has been providing researchers, scholars, and practitioners with timely and substantive information on the critical issues facing higher education. Each monograph presents a definitive analysis of a higher education problem or issue, based on a thorough synthesis of significant literature and institutional experiences. Topics range from planning to diversity and multiculturalism, to performance indicators, to curricular innovations. The mission of the Series is to link the best of higher education research and practice to inform decision making and policy. The reports connect conventional wisdom with research and are designed to help busy individuals keep up with the higher education literature. Authors are scholars and practitioners in the academic community. Each report includes an executive summary, review of the pertinent literature, descriptions of effective educational practices, and a summary of key issues to keep in mind to improve educational policies and practice.

The Series is one of the most peer reviewed in higher education. A National Advisory Board made up of ASHE members reviews proposals. A National Review Board of ASHE scholars and practitioners reviews completed manuscripts. Six monographs are published each year and they are approximately 120 pages in length. The reports are widely disseminated through Jossey-Bass and John Wiley & Sons, and they are available online to subscribing institutions through Wiley InterScience (http://www.interscience.wiley.com).

Call for Proposals

The ASHE Higher Education Report Series is actively looking for proposals. We encourage you to contact one of the editors, Dr. Kelly Ward (kaward@wsu.edu) or Dr. Lisa Wolf-Wendel (lwolf@ku.edu), with your ideas.

Women's Status in Higher Education

Recent Titles

ASHE HIGHER EDUCATION REPORT

ORDER FORM SUBSCRIPTION AND SINGLE ISSUES

DISCOUNTED BACK ISSUES:

Use this form to receive 20% off all back issues of *ASHE Higher Education Report*.
All single issues priced at **$23.20** (normally $29.00)

TITLE	ISSUE NO.	ISBN
_____	_____	_____
_____	_____	_____
_____	_____	_____

*Call 888-378-2537 or see mailing instructions below. When calling, mention the promotional code JBNND
to receive your discount. For a complete list of issues, please visit www.josseybass.com/go/aehe*

SUBSCRIPTIONS: (1 YEAR, 6 ISSUES)

☐ New Order   ☐ Renewal

U.S.	☐ Individual: $174	☐ Institutional: $265
CANADA/MEXICO	☐ Individual: $174	☐ Institutional: $325
ALL OTHERS	☐ Individual: $210	☐ Institutional: $376

*Call 888-378-2537 or see mailing and pricing instructions below.
Online subscriptions are available at www.onlinelibrary.wiley.com*

ORDER TOTALS:

Issue / Subscription Amount: $ _____

Shipping Amount: $ _____
(for single issues only – subscription prices include shipping)

Total Amount: $ _____

SHIPPING CHARGES:

First Item	$5.00
Each Add'l Item	$3.00

*(No sales tax for U.S. subscriptions. Canadian residents, add GST for subscription orders. Individual rate subscriptions must
be paid by personal check or credit card. Individual rate subscriptions may not be resold as library copies.)*

BILLING & SHIPPING INFORMATION:

☐ **PAYMENT ENCLOSED:** *(U.S. check or money order only. All payments must be in U.S. dollars.)*

☐ **CREDIT CARD:**   ☐ VISA   ☐ MC   ☐ AMEX

Card number _____ Exp. Date_____

Card Holder Name_____ Card Issue # _____

Signature _____ Day Phone_____

☐ **BILL ME:** *(U.S. institutional orders only. Purchase order required.)*

Purchase order # _____
          Federal Tax ID 13559302 • GST 89102-8052

Name_____

Address_____

Phone_____ E-mail_____

Copy or detach page and send to: **John Wiley & Sons, PTSC, 5th Floor
                                      989 Market Street, San Francisco, CA 94103-1741**

Order Form can also be faxed to: **888-481-2665**

PROMO JBNND